Rewriting the Word

Recent Titles in
Contributions in Women's Studies

Rewriting the Word

American Women Writers and the Bible

Amy Benson Brown

Contributions in Women's Studies,
Number 172

GREENWOOD PRESS
Westport, Connecticut • London

Library of Congress Cataloging-in-Publication Data

Brown, Amy Benson.
    Rewriting the word : American women writers and the Bible / Amy Benson Brown.
        p.   cm.—(Contributions in women's studies, ISSN 0147–104X ; no. 172)
    Includes bibliographical references and index.
    ISBN 0–313–30865–9 (alk. paper)
    1. American literature—Women authors—History and criticism.
2. Christianity and literature—United States—History. 3. Feminism and literature—United States—History. 4. Women and literature—United States—History. 5. Religion and literature. 6. Bible—In literature. I. Title. II. Series.
PS147.B76   1999
810.9′3822—dc21   98–37718

British Library Cataloguing in Publication Data is available.

Library of Congress Catalog Card Number: 98–37718
ISBN: 0–313–30865–9
ISSN: 0147–104X

First published in 1999

Greenwood Press, 88 Post Road West, Westport, CT 06881
An imprint of Greenwood Publishing Group, Inc.
www.greenwood.com

Printed in the United States of America

The paper used in this book complies with the Permanent Paper Standard issued by the National Information Standards Organization (Z39.48–1984).

10 9 8 7 6 5 4 3 2

Copyright Acknowledgments

The author and publisher gratefully acknowledge permission for use of the following material:

Excerpts from "A Prayer to Eve" and "For My Aunt Mary" from *Little Girls in Church* by Kathleen Norris, copyright © 1995. Reprinted by permission of the University of Pittsburgh Press.

For my mother and father

Prayer to Eve

Mother of fictions
and of irony,
help us to laugh.

Mother of science
and the critical method,
keep us humble.

Muse of listeners,
hope of interpreters,
inspire us to act.

Bless our metaphors,
that we might eat them.

Help us to know, Eve,
the one thing we must do.

Come with us, muse of exile,
mother of the road.

Kathleen Norris, Little Girls in Church

Contents

Preface

In the beginning of American feminist biblical revision was the Word, the same Word that brought the Puritans to these shores and that so decidedly shaped American literature. In the beginning also was American women's imaginative grappling with the meaning of the Word and the significance of their own words. In my attempt to write a genesis for feminist biblical revision in America—to write a story of origin for the confrontation with the Bible that this study explores—I cannot disentangle text from interpretation.

All such stories of origin, of course, are mythic. The reality is that this story begins in medias res, in the middle, where American women writers find themselves struggling with a Bible that they inherit but that never seems as monovocal or monolithic as church officials and policy makers have suggested. Even defining exactly what the Bible signifies for writers is a dicey proposition. The text of the King James Version or the Revised Standard, for example, coexists in our cultural imagination with popularizations, bastardizations, literary echoes, and the long and complicated history of conflicting theological interpretations. For instance, the opening of this preface—"in the beginning . . . was the Word"—actually echoes St. John's gloss on Genesis, rather than the opening of the Bible. Confronting the Bible in American culture has always meant confronting the mix of "memory and desire" that seemed so cruel to T. S. Eliot. For American women writers, this very ambiguity of meaning often has opened an intriguing pathway to their creation of their own words. Perhaps the most accurate story of origin I can offer for feminist biblical revision is what was "in the beginning" for me as a reader of women reading the Bible.

Each day of my grandmother's life began with an hour of Bible reading and prayer. While I savored the Southern food that she cooked without recipes and enjoyed the clothes that she sewed without patterns, her biblical interpretation always appeared to me to follow closely the prescriptions of church leaders in the rural Protestant community where we lived. During my graduate study, I returned to that community to attend my grandmother's funeral. As a member of her Bible study group offered condolences, she shared with me how much she had always enjoyed my grandmother's original and unique ways of reading the Bible. Something clicked for me at that moment.

Despite my grief, or perhaps because of it, I made a connection between the contradictory and sometimes subversive ways that women alone and in small groups read the Bible and the conflicting "hermeneutics," or principles of biblical interpretation, that characterize the writings of the women authors I studied. This glimpse into the dynamics of a small church reading group also suggested to me the sources and significance of the confrontations with the Bible that occur in the works of a great many American women poets and novelists. The latter decades of the twentieth century have witnessed a burst of women's writing about the Bible from various perspectives and disciplines. I started to investigate what feminist women, in particular, find in this ur-text of patriarchy. Thus, this study began with a question: Why do women writers who cannot claim the Bible as their Word—that is, as their spiritual or linguistic inheritance—engage that ancient text in their poetry and fiction? If I had to collapse their individual stories into one story about American literary history, it would sound something like this.

The story of feminist revision of the Bible in America is a story of authority, power, fear, and ambition. It is not the familiar legend of the genius who creates, like God, out of nothing. It is the story of women whose ambition is twin to their anxiety about writing, about what it means to be a woman writer in a masculine-dominated culture. This is not the anxiety of influence—not the fear that she will fail to be original—but the fear caused by the knowledge that she *is* original. Furthermore, that which marks her as different also consigns her to the realm of the silent, that realm that philosophical and literary traditions have designated as before or beyond language. The shocking development in the plot of this story is that the text to which these writers turn for help is the very same text that most famously inscribes these notions about gender and authority. The Bible is the text these writers must confront, not only because it outlines their demons, but because it releases them. Even authors as different as Emily Dickinson and Gloria Naylor create a literary dialogue with the Bible that consistently engenders a new "Word"—an alternative story of inheritance, entitlement, and authority. In their biblical revision, these women construct a Bible that much resembles the Eve of Kathleen Norris's poem, a "mother of fictions" capable of blessing the "metaphors" that the writers both create and consume in the production of their own authority.

Acknowledgments

This study contends that audience is crucial to women's writing, especially for those who would challenge the canon, and my efforts here were greatly facilitated by various audiences. My sincerest thanks go to Alicia Ostriker for her example as a teacher and mentor and for her unflagging support during the many years in which this project took shape. Martine Brownley, similarly, was an attentive listener and invaluable supporter. Kathy Crown, Linda Wagner-Martin, and Crystal Woods also provided acute commentary on parts of the manuscript, as did many audience members at various conferences on women's literature and religion in recent years. Sheila Hassel Hughes and Kim Whitehead patiently endured poetic versions of some of this material, even as my students helped me to approach it pedagogically. I appreciate my editor, Elisabetta Linton, for her commitment to this book. My greatest thanks must go to the people who supported me during the seemingly endless years of graduate work when this project was conceived: my parents, James and Linda Brown, and my partner, Brian Mendelsohn.

The Politics and Poetics of Biblical Revision and Contemporary Women's Poetry

Rewriting the Covenant of Literary Authority

My life is a page ripped out of a holy book and part of the first line is missing.

—Adrienne Rich, "Poem of Women"

Haunted by a sense of alienation from a "holy book," any of several generations of American women writers could have penned these words that Rich adapted from Kadia Molodovsky in 1968.[1] Neither alienation nor nostalgia for a lost past, of course, is peculiarly American. What makes these lines revealing of American feminist biblical revision is the fact that the "holy book" played such a prominent role in the foundation of our culture and literary tradition. And submerged in the very beginnings of that tradition are two Puritan women who can be seen as the "first lines" of the pattern that would become feminist biblical revision.

In 1650, when her brother-in-law published a volume of her poems without her permission, Anne Bradstreet became the first American poet. The speaker of Bradstreet's more intimate verses often presents herself in relation to family: first, as the dutiful daughter of a Puritan father who was prominent in the establishment of the Massachusetts Bay Colony; second, as the affectionate partner of her husband, who eventually became governor of the colony; and finally, as the mother of eight flesh and blood children and of American poetry. She casts herself as a humble mother of literature, protesting that her "blushing" was "not small" when her "rambling brat (in print)" did "return." Despite such frequent expressions of humility, Bradstreet produced a body of work that stands "obnoxious to each carping tongue / Who says my hand a needle better fits." For this audacity and for her frank and "delightful" portraits of what it was like to keep "house at the edge of the wilderness," both contemporary feminist poets and conservative scholars remember her.[2]

As a first line in the history of American poetry, particularly in the history of women's writing, Bradstreet represents the idea that in the beginning of American letters was a woman.[3] Discovering a female figure at the beginning of a literary tradition famous for its masculine icons of achievement is key to understanding what becomes a pattern in feminist biblical revision. As we will see, nineteenth- and twentieth-century women's revisionary readings of the Bible often focus on the recovery of a lost or buried originating female figure. While Bradstreet certainly offers a literary corollary to that inaugurating maternal image, her own engagement of the Bible largely reflects Puritan orthodoxy. Her devotional and meditative poems reveal the common Puritan themes of the necessity of submitting to divine will, understanding personal loss as divine chastisement, and redemption in the afterlife of perfect union with God.[4] Another Puritan "Anne," a contemporary of Bradstreet's whose religious infamy probably exceeded the other's poetic fame, offers quite a different "first line" for feminist biblical revision in America.

When Anne Hutchinson first came to Boston in 1634, she acted as midwife and spiritual adviser to women. Soon, however, the weekly prayer meetings she conducted began to draw larger groups and challenge the prevailing Puritan understanding of the implications of the covenant of grace between God and the chosen ones, the "elect." Hutchinson's followers' radical privileging of grace over works as evidence of individuals' status within the church was seen as antinomian heresy and ignited a struggle that shook the Puritan community to its core. A few years after she was "excommunicated and exiled," she settled in the wilds of New York, where she was killed along with most of her family in a Native American raid.[5] As Amy Lang has argued, Hutchinson's longevity and power as a figure in the American literary imagination derives from the "uncomfortable" closeness of her antinomian heresy, which exalted the sanctity of individual revelation, to the American tradition of individualism and self-expression.[6]

As another "first line" of feminist biblical revision, Hutchinson represents the beginning of a pattern of radical questioning of the dominant structures of religious interpretation. Though Anne Bradstreet was celebrated by her community while Anne Hutchinson was banished, both Annes represent a usurpation of biblically based structures of authority. The spirits of the dutiful daughter of Puritanism and the "American Jezebel"[7] enliven the biblical revision of the women who follow them. Together, these two first lines of the story of feminist biblical revision help to explain Adrienne Rich's stubborn questioning of the meaning of covenant two centuries later.

After probing the roots of "Monotheism" in the desert, the roots of domination and survival, ritual and song, Rich wonders if "this" is "for us," "with whom, and where, is the covenant?"[8] The power of the word "covenant" in organizing culture, as well as its long history of emendation and reconstruction, render it an effective symbol not only of biblical contracts, but also of other political and representational structures.[9] Thus, Rich's questioning of the terms of the covenant between God and humanity can symbolize the negotiations of all women writers who engage the Bible in a reconstruction of their literary inheritance and the authority of their own word. Literally, though,

Rich here certainly refers to God's covenant with Abraham, the foundation of the relationship between the divinity and humanity. As Hutchinson's story illustrates, "covenant" also has particular significance in the American literary landscape since America was originally imagined as a new Israel or Eden. One of earliest types of discourse to emerge in America in fact concerns a reinterpretation of covenant. The jeremiad is a type of sermon that Puritan ministers used as an exposition of the terms of God's covenant with the new nation.

Properly understood, feminist biblical revision is a type of literary discourse somewhat analogous to the jeremiad as Perry Miller defined it: a biblically based literary genre with its own linguistic conventions.[10] Although feminist biblical revision is not a rant, it is, like the jeremiad, an exposition, a reading, of the covenant between divine and human authority. Though the jeremiad and modern feminist revisPion both blend politics and poetics in rereading the Bible, the differences between the two genres are telling. While the purpose of the Puritan ministers' jeremiad was to call a sinful nation back to orthodoxy, feminist biblical revision questions the very foundations of biblical and literary orthodoxy. Furthermore, the authors of feminist biblical revision, unlike the ministers who delivered jeremiads, are outside the sacred spaces of churches and synagogues. Therefore, their redefining of "covenant" reaches beyond the biblical roots of the idea of covenant to encompass larger, sometimes secular constructions of authority.

To understand the significance of this genre, one must understand that these texts are not only talking back to the Bible, but talking to a larger audience as well. Reenvisioning the Bible, then, is simultaneously an effort to reconstruct the cultural context where interpretation occurs. Like the nineteenth-century popular writers Jane Tompkins studies, biblical revisionists have "designs" on textual and cultural traditions that have had designs on them.[11] Thus, feminist biblical revision provides another chapter in the ongoing "cultural work" of American literature. While we pay attention to these writers' aesthetic achievements and inventions, we should not lose sight of their "attempts to redefine the social order."[12]

We should also note, however, that while some examples of feminist biblical revision seem to offer themselves as alternatives to both literary and theological canons, the revisionist enterprise is actually fundamental to both traditions. Perhaps the greatest theme of American literature has been the construction and reconstruction of "a usable literary past."[13] That reconstruction has often involved both the Bible and the revered texts of the literary canon. Thus, H.D.'s, Plath's, and Naylor's biblical dialogues are also conversations with Homer and Freud, Eliot and Yeats, and Hughes and Hurston. This conversation with both sacred and secular textual precursors is inevitable given the crucial position of the Bible in the canonical literary heritage. Furthermore, the baptism of nineteenth-century American authors in the language of the King James Version, combined with the urge to define an original American voice and vision, particularly disposes American literature to revisionist quests.

Revision is inherent in biblical tradition as well as in literary tradition, though that fact is often ignored or masked. The characteristics that render the Bible vulnerable to reinterpretation—namely, its diversity and internal contradictions—are commonplaces of mainstream biblical scholarship and a treasure trove for literary criticism of the Bible.[14] Before we celebrate the Bible as the arch example of an "open work," we must recognize that the long process of its composition and redaction records the successes and failures of particular political agendas in various eras.[15] Repeated references in the early books of the Bible to the infidelity of the Israelites to a single God, for example, suggest the culture's resistance to abandoning the pantheism and fertility-based religious practices of other Near Eastern cultures. A key strategy for propagating monotheism may have been the absorption and revision of images and symbols from the sacred stories of the older religions. Robert Alter even suggests that the sense of an underlying unity in the Bible is strengthened by the text's "allusiveness" to "non-Hebrew ancient Near Eastern texts," as those older stories were recast within the Bible's own "corpus."[16] Thus, we can see that the only possible "unbelated author"—that is, God as presented in Genesis—is actually "the original exemplar of literary belatedness."[17]

Several feminist critics have recently wondered if the "anxiety of influence" haunting Genesis is a masculine fear of feminine creativity and generativity. Modifying Freud's speculation about a possible murder of Moses by his followers as the repressed content of biblical narrative, Alicia Ostriker hypothesizes that the Bible's repressed content is not "the slain Father but the slain (and immortal) Mother."[18] Working her way back to the Bible through another father of modern thought, Christine Froula similarly concludes that Milton's creation scene reveals that "the repression of the mother is the genesis of Genesis."[19] Whatever the historical accuracy of this idea, I am interested in it as the central critical fiction or fantasy of feminist biblical revisionists. The elision of the divine feminine in Genesis is an especially potent symbol of what Margaret Homans characterizes as the "overt murder" of the mother that enables the foundation of the whole symbolic order.[20] Historically speaking, it is also apparent why twentieth-century women writers, still marked by the legacy of the nineteenth-century interpretations of Paul's injunction against female speech, would search for an alternative myth of origins that would not gender Logos—the generative power of language—as exclusively male.

"Lot's Wife": Defining the Genre

A closer look at a typical example of feminist biblical revision will illustrate the general principles and the conventions that mark this genre. The character of Celia Gilbert's 1983 poem "Lot's Wife" is particularly interesting because she both performs revision and symbolizes it in her act of looking back.[21]

The voice Gilbert gives to this speechless character, infamous for her refusal to obey Lot and the Lord and her subsequent transformation into a pillar of salt, redirects the reader's understanding of that Genesis narrative. The perspective of Lot's wife, as Gilbert imagines it, mistrusts the "angels of Lord" and their mission, just as it indicts Lot for his willingness to sacrifice his virgin daughters to a rapacious mob to save the angels. Lot's wife's voice and perspective, however, are not the sole agents of revision in the poem. By flanking the voice of Lot's wife with excerpts from Genesis and from texts about the dropping of the atomic bomb, Gilbert requires the reader to connect the destruction of Sodom and Gomorrah with the modern holocausts of Hiroshima and Nagasaki. Thus, readers are obliged to reevaluate the moral implications of the ancient myth in terms of recent cultural memory. Not only does "Lot's Wife" satisfy Rich's definition of revision by requiring us to "enter an old text from a new critical direction" and "know it differently,"[22] but it is representative of feminist biblical revision specifically in several ways.

First, the voice given to the woman silenced in the ancient story is shaped by what feminist theologians call a "hermeneutics of suspicion," a fundamental mistrust of political hierarchies and values embodied in the traditional text. The knowledge of good and evil that Eve originally consumed becomes for Lot's wife "more sour than the apple," revealing God to be a "behemoth in love with death." This refusal to "live God's lies" echoes Sylvia Plath's chilling leveling of God with the devil—"Herr God, Herr Lucifer"—and, more distantly, Emily Dickinson's indictment of the "Father" as "Burglar, Banker." While this hermeneutics of suspicion is almost always accompanied and complicated by other ways of reading biblical texts, this political critique is basic to biblical revision and distinguishes it from other literary uses of the Bible. For example, while the trenchant irony of Mrs. Turpin's vision of the meek's inheritance of the earth in Flannery O'Connor's short story "Revelation" reveals a deep distrust of Southern culture, it does not challenge biblical authority. Similarly, Eliot's "Four Quartets" beautifully turn and return to the language of the Bible and the Anglican liturgy without ever dislocating the orthodox significations of the phrases he echoes.[23] In contrast, all the texts included in this study overtly seek to alter the cultural signification or traditional reading of biblical images, plots, and themes.[24]

"Lot's Wife" represents another basic trait of biblical revisionist literature in that it foregrounds something previously invisible but always latent in the original narrative.[25] While Gilbert's poem conforms to the plot of the Genesis episode, she expands the field of credible interpretations by asserting that Lot's wife's transformation into a pillar was an act of her own will. Committed to the memory of her community, she wills her "body, transfixed by grief, / to rise in vigil / over the ashen cities." Gilbert's poem therefore alerts readers to the possibility of another story, another interpretative pathway, that has been obscured by the traditional framing of this episode.[26]

Furthermore, "Lot's Wife" underscores the shaping power of language itself. Biblical revisionists probe a variety of feminist and postmodern linguistic issues, but here the tendency to underline a question of language determines the architecture of the poem. The voice of Lot's wife, unheard for centuries, does not emerge with the universal "I" of dramatic monologue; instead, she speaks intertextually with the quotations from Genesis and the modern bomber pilot. The deconstruction of traditional interpretation effected by this juxtaposition of different voices requires a concomitant recognition that Lot's wife's perspective also rises from a particular political and historical location. Here, we can see the tendency of revisionists not only to undercut the authority of traditionally powerful patriarchal institutions, like the Bible or the U.S. military, but also to question the grounds of authority itself.

Many revisionist texts foreground the dialogic basis of their authorship by building a formal correlative of the dialogue into their text. Gilbert's juxtaposition of quotations, mimetic of a discordant dialogue, achieves precisely this effect. In other works, fairy tales or aspects of popular culture often recontextualize a biblical episode and reveal a larger cultural pattern. Consider the conclusion of Anne Sexton's sequence of poems "The Jesus Papers" (self-reflexively titled, of course, "The Author of the Jesus Papers Speaks"):

> Then God spoke to me and said:
> Here. Take the gingerbread lady
> and put her in your oven.
> When the cow gives blood
> and the Christ is born
> we must all eat sacrifices.
> We must all eat beautiful women.[27]

Images from Christianity, psychoanalytical dream analysis, and Grimm's fairy tales coalesce here in a mythopoeic statement about gender and culture. Revisionists' frequent blending of biblical narrative with other literary works, myths, or folklore undercuts the pretension of any story to ahistoric, abstract, or universal truth even as this strategy of collage foregrounds the fact of the text's own construction.

These literary strategies combine with the overtly politicized engagement of the Bible to mark these writers as some of the most original talents since Eliot wrote his famous essay on the importance of tradition to originality. While Eliot's conservative political beliefs and conventional uses of Christian tradition may make him an unlikely pater of the feminist revisionist movement, such are the paradoxes of twentieth-century literary history.[28] A careful reading of "Tradition and the Individual Talent" reveals that Eliot's understanding of the writer's relation to history and the literary canon sparks precisely the kind of creative dialogue with the past that characterizes feminist biblical revision.

Revisionists' struggles with the history of mainstream biblical interpretation and its iterations throughout literary and popular culture demonstrate that they obtain their inheritance from tradition "by great labor," as Eliot observes is necessary.[29] Furthermore, their work testifies to the formative influence of the "dead writers" on all that they know. For example, although Lucille Clifton eventually posits a mutually effecting relationship with history, her poem "i am accused of tending to the past . . ." opens by declaring that "the past was waiting for me / when I came." But for Clifton it is the past, not the newly arrived speaker, that is the "monstrous unnamed baby" that the speaker must suckle and name.[30] Eliot's assertion that an understanding of the significance of tradition "is what makes a writer most acutely conscious of his place in time, of his own contemporaneity"[31] points to another characteristic of biblical revisionism: it is historically bidirectional, engaged both with timeless ancient work and with the temporal moment of its own composition. Again, "Lot's Wife" reflects this model. The critique of patriarchal culture that allows Lot to offer his daughters as sacrifice to a rapacious mob and the obliteration of a whole community is inseparable from the critique of the contemporary patriarchal military culture that sanctions the obliteration of whole Japanese cities. An initial definition, immediately following the title "Lot's Wife," pointedly renames the title character as "hibakusha," the Japanese designation for those afflicted by the bombing of Hiroshima and Nagasaki. This historical double vision relates to the dual focus of feminist biblical revision. While revisionist works ultimately aspire to alter the "relations, proportions, and values of each work of art" toward Eliot's "ideal order,"[32] this literary movement also seeks to revise the social and representational covenant—the symbolic order that places the feminine outside of language.

Of course, feminist revisionists modify as well as appropriate Eliot's model. A crucial difference is the biblical revisionists' insistence on the power of writers and critics to shape our conception of the ideal order. Eliot's use of the passive voice in his formulation of the perpetual modification of the order implies the existence of an eternal canon prior to and independent of the judgment of human agents: critics, teachers, publishers. While Eliot speaks of the "responsibilities" placed on the contemporary writer by his or her ability to alter the ideal order,[33] he elides the effects of critical institutions (and institutionalized critics) in shaping the order.

Revisionists also reject Eliot's final insistence on a strict separation of the "man who suffers" from the "mind which creates."[34] The assertion of feminism in the 1970s that "the personal is political" extends to revisionist poetry and fiction even as the mingling of feminism and postmodernism in the 1980s has complicated our understanding of both the personal and the political. As Ostriker has noted, those who would "steal the language" insistently modify Wallace Stevens's understanding of the imagination by asserting that "God and the imagination and my body are one."[35]

This focus on the corporeal as an agent or shaper of knowledge is another characteristic of biblical revision. Critics who dismiss the attention to the personal, the domestic, and the bodily as merely confessional misunderstand the works' critique of epistemological and literary conventions. Moreover, as "Lot's Wife" demonstrates, placing the corporeal at center stage often calls forth a concomitant recognition of the material effects of history. Certainly, the historical events of World War II and their material aftermath pertain to the poem's critique of asymmetrical gender relations. Furthermore, the broken body of the poem's form intensifies our awareness of the destroyed flesh of the victims of war. The fragmented, collage structure of Gilbert's poem enables the telling comparison of the bodies of the young girls of Sodom who are "shy" but "sturdy" with the journalistic description of the flayed victims of the atomic blast: "'girls, very young girls, not only with their clothes torn off but with their skin peeled off as well'" (66).

Finally, "Lot's Wife" serves as an appropriate introduction to this study because it reflects two thematic concerns centered on home and war. "Revision," broadly defined, could include any reconstruction of a textual "past" from any political perspective.[36] However, feminist biblical revisionists' overarching redesignation of authority, both wrenching and subtle, is often tied to an awareness of cultural liminality, an interpretative position on the borders between the culturally sanctioned and the unimagined. Such a position gives the writer a critical perspective on the center and forces her to choose a community, a territory, a home. Lot's wife's heroism and death result from her inability to turn away from her home community. And as we saw above, a focus on the material body seems to lead inevitably to a focus on the mortal body. The vulnerability, as well as the vision, accompanying the author's liminal position often merges with this heightened awareness of the corporeal to create a concern for what most threatens the body—war— both as organized military conflict and as a trope for more intimate or domestic violence.

One significant characteristic of many revisionist works that "Lot's Wife" does not reflect is the strategic use of humor. The manifestation of humor varies from gentle, if mischievous, mocking—as when Sexton finds the "gods of world" in the "lavatory" and, delighted, "locks the door"—to the bitter irony of Plath's Lady Lazarus's parodic performance for the "peanut-crunching crowd." Humor is always a tool of critique particularly available to the disenfranchised, the writer exiled or walking the border of a literary homeland.[37]

As Luce Irigaray has suggested, though, the expression of women's own pleasure is specifically forbidden or devalued precisely because it gives the lie to the narcissistic, masculine "economy of the same."[38] To do justice to women authors, we must "listen with another ear" because, if we could discern a feminine desire, it would not "speak with the same language as a man's."[39] The postmodern play that characterizes some recent biblical revision, like Naylor's *Bailey's Cafe*, even suggests that this pleasure may be an essential tool for changing the articulation of gender in the dominant culture, represented in the marriage of the literary ideal order and the cultural economy of the same.

Theorizing Feminist Biblical Revision

Theorizing the field of feminist biblical revisionism is particularly complex because many of its texts arise from the intersection of theology and literature. Although feminist and womanist theologies sometimes parallel or complement these texts, my analysis draws largely on literary theory and criticism because I believe that the history of biblical revision has been driven by a changing understanding of the cultural function of language and the relationship of the writer to language. H.D.'s turn to biblical, Greek, and Near Eastern myths, for example, is part of the modernist drive to "shore the fragments" of literary history against our cultural "ruin," just as her revision is enabled by modernist linguistic experimentation.

As modernism shaded into postmodernism, shifting debates about language, authority, and interpretation presented some liberating possibilities but simultaneously threatened revisionists' tentative constructions of authority. As Teresa DeLauretis has noted, much postmodern theory either ignores gender or inevitably discovers the female subject "hopelessly caught in patriarchal swamps or stranded somewhere between the devil and the deep blue sea."[40] The well-known debate in the 1980s about Roland Barthes's "death of the author" is a good example of the way an argument apparently unconcerned with gender can collaborate in the maintenance of the status quo. While feminist revisionists of course could capitalize on the literary power vacuum this argument creates by shifting responsibility for textual signification from the historical author to the writerly reader, many feminists remain deeply committed to the significance of the woman writer's historical "signature." Like Nancy Miller, many revisionists read postmodern philosophies with the same hermeneutics of suspicion with which they approach the Bible, but they nevertheless take inspiration from the intense Derrid-

ian play with signification, the Barthesian broadening of responsibility for authorship, and the Foucaultian investigation of
the shaping power of institutions and historical location on the
construction of identities. Thus, feminist biblical revision is
fundamentally a modern (and sometimes a postmodern) under-
taking.

A survey of the central critical paradigms most useful to an
analysis of revisionist works shows that much feminist theo-
rization on the relation of twentieth-century women writers to
canonical literary history also pertains to their engagement of
the Bible, partly because the Bible is woven into the literary
canon and partly because the Bible often symbolizes the ultimate form of patriarchal textual authority. To clarify the contribution of different feminist critics to an analysis of biblical
revision, I have broken down the principal theories that
emerged in the 1980s into four models or ways of conceptual-
izing the work of revision: (1) temporal comparative, (2) layered textual, (3) psychoanalytic, and (4) theological. Of course,
these models overlap one another in various ways; insights
from psychoanalysis, for example, inform almost all of them to
some degree. This breakdown of these intersecting theories
into separate categories is meant only to illuminate the principal contributions and emphases of each approach.

The clearest formulation of what I am calling the "temporal
comparative" model is Ellen Friedman's application of Jean-
François Lyotard's theory of the "missing contents" of modern
literature.[41] Lyotard contends that modern literature yearns for
the master narratives that once provided meaning but are no
longer representable and function as the literature's "missing
contents." Friedman, however, does not find this to be the case
in twentieth-century women's writing. Instead, she contends
that the missing contents of women's writing are located in the
future, in the "not yet presented," rather than in a nostalgia for
the unpresentable past. With a comparative reading of revisions of Cervantes's *Don Quixote* by Jorge Luis Borges and by
Kathy Acker, Friedman shows how gender redirects the loca-

tion of the "missing contents of modernity." Both the male-
and female-signed texts contain the idea of the unrepre-
sentable; yet Borges's novel yearns for what is past while
Acker's anticipates what is to come.[42] Friedman's method here
demonstrates two fundamental assumptions of much of feminist literary criticism in the vein of Sandra Gilbert and Susan
Gubar's foundational work: that we can better understand the
problematic relation of gender and literary tradition (1) by
comparing texts by male and female authors and noting the differences, and (2) by paying attention to the differences that are
apprehendable when these works are examined against the
backdrop of chronological history.[43] Using this model, we
could map the evolving relation of gender and literature
against a historical grid.

This temporal comparative approach may lend itself more
readily to fiction than to poetry because the plots of fiction
often assume a certain time line. Rachel Blau Duplessis's work
*Writing Beyond the Ending: The Narrative Strategies of Twentieth-
Century Women Writers*, also posits a primarily linear movement from nineteenth- to twentieth-century texts and traces
the efforts of women writers to break problematic plotlines.
Duplessis finds women writers "breaking the sentence" of the
internalized laws of gender ideology and then "breaking the sequence" of the conventional plots that have allowed only marriage or death as the endings of women's narratives.[44] Although
this narrative-based theory may lend itself more obviously to
analysis of fiction, it certainly works across genres. To return to
"Lot's Wife," for example, we can see a sharp break in the "sentence" mandating respect for biblical authority in her indictment of "God's lies," while the "sequence," the story, remains
unbroken since the poem, like the Genesis narrative, depicts
Lot's wife's final transformation into a statue.

While Friedman's and Duplessis's work clearly demonstrates
the valuable critical insights offered by this approach, no ana-
lytic paradigm can reveal the whole scene of the troubled relation of gender and literary history because every approach

necessarily shapes the picture as it illuminates it. The blind
spot of the temporal comparative model is that it is inherently
teleological. The end that this model implicitly posits is often a
happy, sometimes even a utopian, one. Behind this model whispers the tremendously appealing hope that the traditional,
problematic constructions of gender and authority are being
overcome and one day will no longer bedevil women's creativity. Although there obviously is a case to be made for the
progress of women's rights in the twentieth century, a faith in
linear progress cannot explain, for instance, why Plath's and
Sexton's letters to the world and God are often more wounded
than Dickinson's. As often as not, the authority these writers
construct through their engagement of the Bible resembles the
furious or sorrowful lament of a disillusioned prophet. Therefore, in addition to tracing the fault lines and ruptures that revisionist works create in literary history, we need to understand
the conflicting dynamics within the works themselves. This
need is answered by what I am calling the "layered textual" approach.

Alicia Ostriker and Marianne Dekoven have both described
the peculiar ways that women's writing has been shaped by ambivalent impulses. Ostriker delineates three intersecting and
sometimes contradictory ways that women poets read and
rewrite the Bible. The first, which was earlier marked as fundamental to revision, is a hermeneutics of suspicion, a profound mistrust of the Bible as a textual emissary of cultural
powers that threaten the woman's autonomy and deny her authority. Like every recognizable example of ideology, however,
the Bible contains gaps and contradictions that, as noted earlier, provide some interpretive flexibility. This play or "give" in
the narrative invites readers' own inventiveness, and from this,
as Ostriker points out, comes the second way that revisionists
read the text: with the hermeneutics of desire. Here, the writer
"eroticizes" the text, "inserting herself into the story by identifying its spiritualities with her own sensualities, and by feminizings of the divine."[45] Perhaps it is the clash of suspicion and

desire in the interpretive moment that necessitates the third way of reading Ostriker describes, the hermeneutics of indeterminacy. This hermeneutic is best seen in "Lot's Wife" in the form of the poem; its architecture of quotations (from Genesis, Lot's wife, and the modern accounts of war) force the reader's awareness of the poem as a "made thing." Though biblical revisions may be "immediately persuasive," they never claim to be the definitive or final "truth"; instead, they posit indeterminate and plural possibilities of signification.[46]

A critical model employing these three, overlapping hermeneutics allows us to perceive the layers of the revisionist text as they both press and symbiotically support one another—thus my designation of it as the layered textual model. That women's textual engagements of the Bible present a more heightened case of the general situation of women writers confronting the canon is underscored by the similarity of Ostriker's hermeneutics to the "sous-ratour" structure that Dekoven has identified as fundamental to modernist writing.[47] While both male and female writers experience the mix of fear, desire, and ambivalence that defines sous-ratour, these responses are differently inflected by gender. While men desire a changed social order, they may fear a possible loss of hegemony; women's desire for change, however, mingles with a fear of retribution for that desire. Dekoven argues that these equal and opposed forces of fear and desire create forms of unresolvable contradiction, the self-canceling "X" of sous-ratour.

The eternally embattled nature of this structure can be seen in the conclusion of "Lot's Wife," as the figure's body "transfixed by grief" keeps eternal "vigil over the ashen cities" (71). The figure's agency, her guardianship of the destroyed community, is inseparable here from the constraint of her statuelike form. Dekoven's speculation that this structure may release the repressed maternal, albeit in vexed and politically ambiguous ways,[48] may also bear on the common quest of biblical revisionism for a female figure of the divine. The influence of feminist theories of psychoanalysis on the layered textual approach of both Dekoven and Ostriker highlights the influence of psychoanalytic theory, the third approach I mentioned earlier, on many of these interpretive rubrics.

Working from psychoanalytic theory, Margaret Homans connects Genesis and the oedipal myth as basic plots underlying the "story of language" and asserts that women's revisions of that story are shaped by their longer period of preoedipal attachment to their mothers.[49] While women enter the masculine realm of the symbolic order, they retain an ability to value the "literal" over the "figurative" that the symbolic order denigrates. Using the psychoanalytic theories of Nancy Chodorow, Homans shows that Jacques Lacan's version of the child's entry into the symbolic order is only the most recent manifestation of a cultural myth that associates the mother with the literal and requires the absence of both for language, which is fundamentally figurative, to signify. Interestingly, Homans suggests that representation for the daughter may "indeed mean presence, not absence"[50] and outlines strategies of "literalization" that women writers practice in an attempt to tell a different story of language. Though Homans culled these strategies from the texts of nineteenth-century British women writers, they also describe many twentieth-century biblical revisionists' efforts to "bear the word." "Lot's Wife," for example, evidences the first strategy of literalization—making it real—by transforming the distant, mythical narrative of the destruction of Sodom into an almost tangible contemporary reality by conflating it with the destruction of Hiroshima. Similarly, Gilbert literalizes the famous figure of Lot's wife by making her a credible representation of a warm, breathing person torn by her links to the people around her.

All three models reviewed thus far (the temporal comparative, the layered textual, and the psychoanalytic) derive from feminist literary criticism and theory. Some feminist theologians, however, have developed ways of reading the Bible that intersect with the strategies of some biblical revision. The four "rhetorics" Elisabeth Schussler-Fiorenza recently has identified as feminist strategies for reading the Bible offer a good example of the fourth model I have proposed for theorizing feminist biblical revision.[51] Schussler-Fiorenza's "rhetorics of liberation" traverse similar territory as the hermeneutics of suspicion by questioning biblical texts as representations of an often misogynist ideology. The "rhetorics of differences" insist on an awareness of the revisionist reader's own ideology and cultural location and may be one of the sources of what I have termed the revisionist's sense of "liminality." As Schussler-Fiorenza stresses, this awareness of plural differences requires attention to identity categories, such as race and class, in addition to gender.

The third rhetoric deals with the contested terrain of the Bible's claim to "truth": like Ostriker's hermeneutics of indeterminacy, Schussler-Fiorenza's "rhetorics of equality" assume biblical truth to be not "given" but "made" by readers. Crucial to her view is the concern of these creative readers for the "well-being" of the larger community, which leads to her final "rhetorics of vision." Here, interrogations of biblical texts spur "religious visions that foster equality, justice, and the logic of the ekklesia rather than the logic of patriarchal domination."[52] "Lot's Wife" seems to offer just such a vision because of its rejection of the ruling power as a "behemoth in love with death" and its reclamation of community in Lot's wife's insistence that "those who died are my children now" (70).

Of course, many biblical revisionists would not define themselves as religious or characterize their works as visionary. Yet the pertinence of feminist theology to some biblical revision underscores the challenge these literary works implicitly pose to the dichotomy between the sacred and the secular. A key contribution of Schussler-Fiorenza's "rhetorics" to an understanding of biblical revision is her assumption that these rereadings of the Bible are oriented toward someone, somewhere. This directedness or rhetorical context highlights a basic aspect of revision that often is buried or beyond the focus of the first three models examined.

Feminist biblical revision is inherently rhetorical: it is speech
intended to persuade an audience. The revisionist's engagement
of the ancient text, in one sense, then, is really a "cover story"
for the writer's conversation with her own culture. In another
sense, though, the audience of revisionist rhetoric is often internalized in the text itself because the writer's address to contemporary readers is inseparable from her address to the
ancient text. As the revisionist text attempts to persuade imagined or actual readers, it also relocates the woman writer's authority by reconstructing the relationship of the feminine to
language. Thus, the revisionist enterprise can be understood
through DeLauretis's formulation of the complicated causality
of the relationship between gender and language: the "construction of gender is the product and the process of both representation and self-representation."[53] This aspect of biblical
revision modifies the subject position from which the woman
writer speaks. In sum, a recognition of the role of rhetoric in
biblical revision emphasizes the writer as first and always a
reader for whom, as Wolfgang Iser contends, the "production
of the meaning" of the ancient text "entails the possibility" that
she may also "formulate" herself and "so discover what had
previously seemed to elude [her] consciousness."[54]

The promise of this self-formulation is nothing other than the
woman writer's "signature." The feminist dialogues with one of
the founding texts of patriarchal culture inscribes a clearly read-
able female signature, which Miller defines as "an icon or em-
blem within" the text that "figures the symbolic and material
process" through which women construct an authority.[55] Study-
ing women's signatures is crucial to both an understanding of
how individuals negotiate the masculine hegemony of literary
culture and to an understanding of the complicated dynamics
within women's literary traditions. Women's reimaginations of
the Bible, furthermore, offer a unique window on the ambigui-
ties of writing from a female subject position because of the
Bible's dual function as a cornerstone of both patriarchal culture
and the Western literary tradition. An overview of feminist bib-

lical revision in contemporary women's poetry can isolate the several types of signatures that later chapters will investigate.

Biblical Revision and the Signatures of Contemporary Women Poets

While biblical references remain common in much contemporary poetry, the subject of this study is a specific type of textual encounter that inscribes the author's own literary authority as it records her transgression of biblical authority. Ostriker's "Meditation in Seven Days," for example, closes with the image of the speaker's own "hand on the latch," poised to open and possess the dreams, the domain, of the biblical father.[56] This "hand," of course, is a shorthand, a metonymic representation of the author's own handwriting that has been writing on and over Genesis through all seven sections of this poem. For Ostriker, this signature is inextricable from a historical quest to excavate a buried or lost female presence. In the matrilineal inheritance of Jewish identity—"If your mother is a Jew, you are a Jew"—she discerns a "residue" of some "archaic power" that has been almost erased. Similarly, Eleanor Wilner suspects that the full story of Sarah, "how God spoke" to her, "how a certain faith / was fractured," is simply "not written in the book."[57] While the signature of many women writers is composed though such investigations of absences and silences, another type of women's signature rewrites biblical characters and plots that continue to resonate loudly and profoundly through modern culture.

"Lot's Wife" offers a clear example of that approach. Kathleen Norris's "For My Aunt Mary" similarly refuses conventional uses of the Bible in figurations of women's identities. To an aunt who committed suicide shortly after giving birth—"diagnosis: 'promiscuous' "—Norris asks:

> Were you a Deborah
> called to battle? Or
> a Magdalene, a witness?[58]

This question actually offers a different "diagnosis," or way of representing Aunt Mary's behavior, by refusing the virgin/whore opposition that such stories frequently invoke. A conventional, even sympathetic, rendering of the aunt's plight, for instance, might cloak the unmarried or "promiscuous" mother in the innocence of the Virgin Mary. But Norris eschews that frame altogether, positioning the aunt instead between Magdalene and Deborah. To come to terms with a woman living and dying outside cultural norms, Norris offers us not the biblical personae of virgin and whore, but that of warrior and witness.

A third type of women's signature forgoes the rescripting of historical or narrative possibilities to interrogate biblical language as language, as an archetype or ancestor of the medium of the writer's own authority. And well might a writer turn to the Bible: the Book of Genesis, like the disciplines of philosophy and psychology, is a source of key assumptions about the relation of gender and authority, what Homans calls the "story of language."[59] In this ur-story of modern culture, all figurative language is identified with the masculine and present even as its meaning is predicated on a feminine ground that is always absent or prior. In *The End of Beauty*, for instance, Jorie Graham repeatedly links the biblical myth of origins with questions of linguistic reference, questions of how words acquire meaning. In "Self-Portrait as the Gesture Between Them [Adam and Eve]," Graham's self-portrait is delineated against the background of Eve's fateful gesture. Sharing the forbidden fruit tears the "fabric" of divine and seamless order; Eve's act is "an opening of the narrow passage" that allows Graham to open the passages of Genesis to reveal them as paths for traveling for the resignification of meaning, as well as worn paths of established reference.[60]

Lucille Clifton, by contrast, is less interested in questions of linguistic reference and more interested in the power conferred or withheld by such ontological myths. In "eve thinking," Clifton quite literally "steals the language" from Adam.[61] While Adam "the clay two-foot / rumbles in his chest / searching for language" to call Eve, she waits and plans "to whisper into his mouth / our names."[62] This subversive revision of the Genesis episode of Adam's naming of earth's creatures reflects Clifton's own appropriation of the Bible, of the "Voice" that Wilner calls "Authority's own."[63] That this appropriation is a subversion is evidenced by Clifton's identification throughout "The Tree of Life" (the sequence in which "eve thinking" appears) with Lucifer, the usurper and fallen angel. Clifton's wordplay with her own name, Lucille, underscores her identification with Lucifer, the "light-bringer," even as it slyly highlights her own signature.[64]

Clifton's cagey pun begs the same question as the title of Graham's "Self-Portrait as the Gesture Between Them [Adam and Eve]": Why are all these women inscribing their signature over, around, and against the Bible? Why in the last century have so many portraits of the artist as a young woman been painted against biblical backdrops? The following chapters examine how various women's signatures emerge through their engagement of the Bible in different historical eras and literary movements: Emily Dickinson's nineteenth-century voice, H.D.'s modernism, Sylvia Plath's and Anne Sexton's confessionalism, and Gloria Naylor's and Toni Morrison's postmodern narratives. By tracing the emergence of these various signatures through history, I hope to reveal not only the development of feminist biblical revision, but also the importance of alternative literary traditions to the constructions of female writing identities.

Notes

1. Adrienne Rich, *The Fact of a Doorframe: Poems Selected and New* (New York: Norton, 1984), 90. In an endnote on page 330, Rich explains this poem "was adapted from the Yiddish with the aid of transliterated versions and prose translations provided by Eliezer Greenberg and Irving Howe" and was first published in their anthology *A Treasury of Yiddish Poetry* (New York: Holt, Rinehart, and Winston, 1969).

2. Anne Bradstreet, *The Works of Anne Bradstreet*, ed. Jeannine Hensley (Cambridge, Mass.: Harvard University Press, 1967); see "The Author to Her Book" and the "Prologue." Adrienne Rich's preface to this volume praises Bradstreet's achievement in light of her circumstances. A very different critic, Alfred Kazin, in *God and the American Writer* (New York: Knopf, 1997), 5, also describes her continuing appeal.

3. Patricia Caldwell, "Why Our First Poet Was a Woman: Bradstreet and the Birth of an American Poetic Voice," *Prospects: An Annual Journal of American Cultural Studies* 13 (1988): 1–35.

4. Alicia Suskin Ostriker, *Stealing the Language: The Emergence of Women's Poetry in America* (Boston: Beacon Press, 1986), 20–21.

5. Amy Schrager Lang, *Prophetic Woman: Anne Hutchinson and the Problem of Dissent in the Literature of New England* (Berkeley: University of California Press, 1987), 5. For a graceful explanation of the problem of the covenant of grace for Hutchinsonians, see Lang's first and second chapters.

6. Ibid., 13–14.

7. Ibid., 17.

8. Adrienne Rich, *Time's Power: Poems, 1985–1988* (New York: Norton, 1989), 25–31.

9. T. S. Eliot's literary "ideal order" and the "symbolic order" of Lacanian psychoanalysis, for example, are other representational structures that, like the biblical covenant, have excluded women or relegated them to a preverbal or silent realm.

10. Perry Miller, *The New England Mind from Colony to Province* (Cambridge, Mass.: Harvard University Press, 1953), 29. Here, Miller proposes "jeremiad" as a literary type.

11. Jane Tompkins, *Sensational Designs: The Cultural Work of American Fiction* (New York: Oxford University Press, 1985).

12. Ibid., xi.

13. Richard Ruland and Malcolm Bradbury, *From Puritanism to Postmodernism: A History of American Literature* (London: Routledge, 1991), 5.

14. What Robert Alter characterizes as a remarkable amount of "heterogeneity" and intertextual "debate" and "play" in the Hebrew Bible (Alter and Frank Kermode, eds., *The Literary Guide to the Bible* [Cambridge, Mass.: Harvard University Press, 1987], 12–14) makes Scripture a veritable "paradise of polysemy" for Ostriker (*Feminist Re-*

vision and the Bible [Cambridge: Blackwell, 1993], 62). Certainly, that kind of narrative plurality is compounded by the multiple accounts of the life of Christ in the Gospels. Walter Reed's recent Bakhtinian reading even asserts that "dialogue" is the "most prominent feature" of this narrative of the conversation between God and humanity (*Dialogues of the Word: The Bible as Literature According to Bakhtin* [Oxford: Oxford University Press, 1993], 12–16). The open-ended nature of dialogism raises the possibility that the text is never complete or final, that its significance is always in some respect shaped by the reader.

15. See Umberto Eco's chapter "The Poetics of the Open Work," in *The Role of the Reader* (Bloomington: Indiana University Press, 1979), 47–66. On the traces of cultural contest in the Bible, see Kermode's essay "The Canon" (in *The Literary Guide*, ed. Alter and Kermode, 600–610) and Mieke Bal's *Death and Dissymmetry: The Politics and Coherence in the Book of Judges* (Chicago: University of Chicago Press, 1988).

16. Alter and Kermode, eds., *The Literary Guide*, 13.

17. Ostriker, *Feminist Revision*, 50.

18. Ibid., 36.

19. Christine Froula, "When Eve Reads Milton: Undoing the Canonical Economy," *Critical Inquiry* 10, no. 2 (1983): 321–347, quote at 337.

20. Margaret Homans, *Bearing the Word: Language and Female Experience in Nineteenth-Century Women's Writing* (Chicago: University of Chicago Press, 1986), 11.

21. Celia Gilbert, *Bonfire* (Cambridge, Mass.: Alice James Books, 1983), 64–71. Subsequent references to Gilbert's "Lot's Wife" are cited parenthetically in the text by page number.

22. Adrienne Rich, *On Lies, Secrets, and Silence: Selected Prose, 1966–1978* (New York: Norton, 1979), 35.

23. Eliot's "Journey of the Magi," however, does offer an unconventional and disturbing perspective on the birth of Christ.

24. This study, of course, can focus on only a few of the works produced by women in the last 150 years that meet this criteria.

25. Ostriker, *Feminist Revision*, 28–29.

26. This episode is commonly framed as an illustration of God's wrath, female irresolution, and/or cultural codes of hospitality.

27. Anne Sexton, *The Complete Poems*, ed. Linda Gray Sexton (Boston: Houghton Mifflin, 1981), 344–345.

28. See Peter Ackroyd's biography of Eliot on his conservatism (New York: Simon and Schuster, 1984).

29. T. S. Eliot, "Tradition and the Individual Talent," in *Selected Prose of T. S. Eliot*, ed. Frank Kermode (New York: Farrar, Straus, and Giroux, 1988), 38.

30. Lucille Clifton, *Quilting: Poems, 1987–1990* (Brockport, N.Y.: BOA Editions Ltd., 1991), 7.

31. Eliot, "Tradition and the Individual Talent," 38.

32. Ibid.

33. Ibid., 39.

34. Ibid., 41.

35. Ostriker, *Stealing the Language*, 220–221.

36. The current issue of Holocaust revisionism, the reactionary political and pseudoacademic movement to deny the historical reality of the slaughter of Jews in World War II, tempted me to invent a new term for the subject of this study. While the women writers engaged in biblical revision often approach the Bible in a mode of critique and mood of social change, their political agendas certainly are not about fostering hate or bigotry. Indeed, the opposite is the case.

37. Ostriker asserts that this tendency of women writers to rewrite "tragedy as farce," to make a joke of the sacred, alienates some critics precisely because it targets the most sacred assumption of traditional literary criticism and Western philosophy: that suffering or tragedy is more significant than pleasure and comedy (*Feminist Revision*, 28–29).

38. Luce Irigaray, *This Sex Which Is Not One* (Ithaca, N.Y.: Cornell University Press, 1985), 77.

39. Ibid., 25–29.

40. Teresa DeLauretis, *Technologies of Gender: Essays on Theory, Film, and Fiction* (Bloomington: Indiana University Press, 1987), 9.

41. See Ellen Friedman, "Where Are the Missing Contents?: (Post)Modernism, Gender, and the Canon," *PMLA* 108, no. 2 (1993): 240–252.

42. Ibid., 242–243.

43. See Sandra Gilbert and Susan Gubar's *No Man's Land: The Place of the Woman Writer in the Twentieth Century* (New Haven, Conn.: Yale University Press, 1988), esp. vol. 1, chap. 1, for a further example of the temporal comparative approach, particularly their focus on a literary "battle of the sexes."

44. Rachel Blau Duplessis, *Writing Beyond the Ending: Narrative Strategies of Twentieth-Century Women Writers* (Bloomington: Indiana University Press, 1985).

45. Ostriker, *Feminist Revision*, 66.

46. Ibid., 66–67.

47. Dekoven elaborates her borrowing of this Derridian term in the introduction and first chapter of *Rich and Strange: Gender, History, Modernism* (Princeton, N.J.: Princeton University Press, 1991).

48. Ibid., 30–36.

49. Homans, *Bearing the Word*, 11.

50. Ibid., 14.

51. Schussler-Fiorenza's definition of the term "revisionist" is more narrow and specific to theology than the definition I have offered as the baseline for this study; see *But She Said: Feminist Practices of Biblical Interpretation* (Boston: Beacon Press, 1992), 23–50.

52. See ibid., 131–132. Literally, the "ekklesia" is the "women-church," but Schussler-Fiorenza uses it throughout *But She Said* as a term for the democratically oriented struggle of religious men and women against patriarchal oppression.

53. DeLauretis, *Technologies of Gender*, 5.

54. Wolfgang Iser, "The Reading Process: A Phenomenological Approach," in *Reader Response Criticism: From Formalism to Post-Structuralism*, ed. Jane Tompkins (Baltimore: Johns Hopkins University Press, 1988), 50–69.

55. Nancy K. Miller, *Subject to Change: Reading Feminist Writing* (New York: Columbia University Press, 1988), 129. Miller stresses here that the signature is not just inscribed in its own text, but is fundamentally intertextual.

56. Alicia Ostriker, *Green Age* (Pittsburgh: University of Pittsburgh Press, 1989), 46–56. Here I wish to acknowledge my profound debt to Ostriker for work on women's writing on the Bible in both her teaching and her criticism. See *Feminist Revision* for lectures, poems, and an interview on these subjects and also *The Nakedness of the Fathers: Biblical Visions and Revisions* (New Brunswick, N.J.: Rutgers University Press, 1994) for a rereading of the Bible in poetic, fantastic, and autobiographic genres.

57. Eleanor Wilner, "Sarah's Choice," in *No More Masks: An Anthology of Twentieth-Century American Women Poets*, ed. Florence Howe (New York: HarperPerennial, 1993), 296–298.

58. Kathleen Norris, *Little Girls in Church* (Pittsburgh, University of Pittsburgh Press, 1995), 14.

59. Homans, *Bearing the Word*, 13.

60. Jorie Graham, *The End of Beauty* (New York: Ecco Press, 1987), 3.

61. See Ostriker, *Stealing the Language,* for a larger discussion of this "theft" of language.

62. Clifton, *Quilting*, 78.

63. Wilner, "Sarah's Choice," 296.

64. Clifton, *Quilting*, 80.

Chapter One

" 'Faith' Is a Fine Invention": Emily Dickinson and H.D.

" 'Faith' Is a Fine Invention": The Nineteenth Century and Modernist Roots of This Dialogue

"Faith" is a fine invention
When Gentlemen can *see*—
But *Microscopes* are prudent
In an Emergency.

—Emily Dickinson (34)[1]

The year 1886 marks a pivotal point in American literary history and in the emerging tradition of feminist biblical revision. In that year, Emily Dickinson died and H.D. was born. While this serendipitous fact of biography suggests a neat demarcation in literary history—the passing of the Victorian to the modern era—the poetry of these two women brooks no such neat division. The correspondences and divergences in Emily Dickinson's and H.D.'s biblically informed poetry lay the groundwork for an examination of twentieth-century women's biblical revision because they reveal the defining issues and characteristics of this trajectory in women's reformulations of the canon.

While Dickinson took varying stances toward the Word of her Puritan fathers, her bracketing of " 'Faith' " as an "invention" by or for "Gentlemen" reflects the strong tendency in her work toward critique of the biblical tradition and protest against divine injustice. This bracketed "Faith" also represents the biblical tradition that H.D. inherited, a faith shuttled into quotation marks by the rise of rationalist discourse, which also figures in Dickinson's poem. The idea of faith was further vexed by H.D.'s modernist belief in classical myth as antidote to cultural ruin and her conflicting awareness as a woman writer of the misogyny woven into the layers of Western tradition, what she called "the palimpsest of past misadventure."[2] Thus, H.D.'s major work of biblical revision, the late modernist epic *Trilogy*, echoes Dickinson's assertion that " 'Faith' is a fine invention" but with a difference: a heavier accent on "invention" to stress that the inherited tradition is constructed by people and available for reinvention.

The shift in literary history from E.D. to H.D. is inextricably bound with social and historical shifts as well. The works of both poets reveal the roots of recent issues of identity politics in nineteenth-century conflicts around gender and representation. In Dickinson's lifetime, mainstream representations of women continued to laud the powerful influence of feminine morality and virtue while insisting that the angel of the house stray no more than a few feet from that graced hearth. Even the association of the "sublime" with poetry, which is so prominent in the works of Emerson and Whitman, was defined in masculine terms.[3] But at the same time, voices from the margins were blending biblical rhetoric with reform to argue for women's intellectual and spiritual equality and for broader education and full political representation. Though Dickinson eschewed the public podium as announcing "one's name" to "an admiring Bog" (288), the speeches and writings of feminist reformers in education, politics, and religion, like Sarah Grimké and Elizabeth Cady Stanton, provide the social backdrop for Dickinson's individual negotiations with the authority of the dominant discourse. Grimké's argument in 1838 that the Bible represents women as intellectually and morally equal to men bolstered, a decade later, calls for women's suffrage at the Seneca Falls Convention. The fact that the biblically informed rhetoric of "the woman question" was closely allied with the rhetoric of abolition also sets in motion another powerful line of representation (and questions of misrepresentation) for twentieth-century biblical revision.[4] Furthermore, the Civil War, fought at least in part to abolish slavery, is only the first in a line of American wars that especially impacted feminist biblical revision. The reformers' public challenges to the Word of the Father in the social and political realms and a reclusive poet's private challenges in the literary realm reflect a similar pressure on the issue of women and representation.

As the telling phrasing of "the woman question" (the general label in the nineteenth century for all discussion of reforms of women's roles) suggests, the very meaning of female identity was under question. Since the interrogation of such a category necessarily occurs within cultural and linguistic systems, the woman question inevitably begs questions of language and representation. A brief comparison of the use of the biblical figure of Eve as a representation of women's identity in the sermon of a popular minister and in a contemporaneous letter by a young Emily Dickinson will illustrate the significance of the Bible in this debate about women's identities.

G. C. Baldwin in 1856 published a series of sermons, titled *Representative Women: From Eve, the Wife of the First, to Mary, the Mother of the Second Adam*, in which he dispenses "practical instruction" about women's ideal roles by analogizing various female biblical figures to positive and negative types of women in society.[5] Baldwin's interpretation of Eve's lesson, in particular, reflects the traditional answer to the woman question. The story of the first mother, as a sort of Everywoman, teaches "the true relation of the sexes" based on Eve's subordinate position to Adam in the order of creation. Baldwin reflects the prevailing articulation of gender in his era when he claims that woman's proper role is that of "helpmeet," her greatest power that of the moral "influence" in the home, and her chief danger an "unchecked desire" to "rise" above the sphere in which "Providence had placed her."[6] This traditional interpretation of Eve, which is one of the best-known ontological narratives of female identity, criminalizes ambition and reflects a key source of the anxiety and dread of punishment that often accompanies the "unchecked desire" for authority by women writers in the twentieth century.

Projects like Baldwin's, although they ostensibly discourage women's authorial ambitions, insist on interpreting the question of women's identity discursively, finding an answer to the woman question in the Word. Despite the fact that Baldwin cheerfully evokes Emerson's *Representative Men* as an inspiration for his own work, he inverts Emerson's reasoning. While Emerson uses actual historical men (like Plato and Shakespeare) to define ideal types of characters (such as the Philosopher and the Poet), Baldwin uses ideal types of women (like Eve and Mary) to define actual historical women (such as those in his congregation on Sunday mornings). In short, Emerson works from the historical to the textual, whereas Baldwin works from the textual to the historical. Baldwin's logic, despite its origins in normative ideology, can lead to an expansion of possibilities for representing women.

Following such reasoning about "representative women" to its logical, if absurd, conclusion, a young Emily Dickinson admits in a letter that: "I have lately come to the conclusion that I am Eve, alias Mrs. Adam. You know there is no account of her death in the Bible, and why am I not Eve?"[7] If the biblical Eve represents actual women that live and walk among us, as ministers like Baldwin claimed, then Dickinson's counterclaim suggests that actual women may bring themselves, their histories and experiences, to fresh interpretations of Eve's character and, by extension, fresh answers to the woman question. Working against the role of Eve in Western literature as "other" to Adam's poetic subjectivity, Dickinson reads her instead as a "prototype for poetic subjectivity."[8] This privileging of the tex-

tual or discursive grounds of identity offers one reason why
women writers from Baldwin's day to the present keep return-
ing to the Word for clues to their own authority, despite biblical interpretations that would restrict or negate that authority.

Dickinson's youthful play with identity in this letter to a
friend hints at the common ground of both her and H.D.'s authority as mature poets. The remainder of this chapter will explore how both poets construct discursive identities through
biblical revision. Despite their differences, three issues that I
will use as rubrics for analysis characterize both Dickinson's
and H.D.'s biblical revison and contribute to a pattern that
continues in more recent biblical revision. Their biblical revision is enabled by and expressed through: (1) a rewriting of
"home," signifying both their actual family homes and their
sense of literary lineage and origins; (2) a rewriting of "war,"
signifying both historical wars and war as a trope for literary
agon; and (3) a rewriting of audience, signifying both their personal audiences and the development of the sense of audience
as the recipient and coauthor of a cultural work.

"My Homesick Eye": Home, Identity, and Vision

Nor could I rise—with You—
Because Your Face
Would put out Jesus'—
That New Grace
Grow plain—and foreign
On my homesick Eye—

                              —Emily Dickinson (640)

The family homes of both Dickinson and H.D. were
strongly associated with biblical tradition. Dickinson's paternal
ancestors were closely tied to New England's Puritan past; her
evangelical grandfather, Samuel Fowler Dickinson, established
Amherst College in their hometown of Amherst, Massachu-

setts, to promote through theocentric education the Puritan dream of a New Jerusalem.[9] In her sessions with Sigmund Freud in the 1930s, H.D. also explicitly connects her hometown, Bethlehem, Pennsylvania, with history of the biblical Bethlehem.[10] Similarly, both families' theological "homes" of origin belonged to special sects: the Dickinsons' Puritan traditions and the Doolittles' Moravian ones.[11] Common to all Protestantism, however, is the use of home as a trope for heaven, or ultimate union with God: death, for instance, is often euphemized as homecoming. The security, the home or "haven," for which H.D. sets her course in *Trilogy* simultaneously evokes the blessings of paradise: "possibly we will reach haven, / heaven" (59).

The trope of a heavenly home inevitably also posits an analogy between divine and mortal families. The biblical Word of God the Father came to life for Dickinson in the voice of her own father, Edward Dickinson, who read from the Bible to his family whenever he was home.[12] While H.D.'s own father was less closely personally associated with the voice of God the Father, her dual fascination with religion and psychoanalytic theory inclined her to symbolize the divine/human relation in terms of Freud's family romance. Throughout *Tribute to Freud*, her memoir of her analysis with Freud that freed her from a writing block and enabled the production of *Trilogy*, H.D. self-consciously figures Freud as a father figure, even as the biblical patriarch Moses.

Even more significantly for Dickinson and H.D., their own fathers were strongly associated with the power of the language and the dominant structures of authority in secular realms. Edward Dickinson devoted himself to sustaining Amherst College and wrote articles advocating some educational opportunities for girls (to better prepare them to be wise mothers, however, not wise writers). In addition to his close identification with the academy, he also was an accomplished lawyer and served in the Massachusetts legislature, where he voted against women's suffrage.[13] In sum, to read Dickinson's father as symbolic of a biblical pater requires a recognition of the metonymic slippage of that symbol. His public career offers a strikingly clear example of how the biblical figure of the Father can readily symbolize the intertwined politics of the different faces of phallic discourse: the power of the Father's Word in the academy, law, government, and religion. Similarly, H.D.'s own father, an astronomy professor, was allied with the academia, while her figurative father, Freud, pioneered one of the most influential phallic discourses of our century, psychoanalysis.

For both poets, the seeming omnipresence of paternal power was thrown into stark relief by the seeming absence of maternal power, which radically destabilized their sense of home, or origin. Dickinson asked of Thomas Wentworth Higginson: "Could you tell me what home is? I never had a mother. I suppose a mother is one to whom you hurry when you are troubled."[14] Biographers have described Dickinson's mother as a very quiet, shy woman who deferred to her husband in all things.[15] H.D. felt similarly "motherless" when she reflected on her own mother's emotional distance and forfeiture of her artistic talent for painting.[16] Ironically, the strong association both poets made between their actual mothers and the running of a household, the supervision and execution of domestic duties, barred an association of maters with an artistic home, a sense of origin and lineage that would authorize their literary vocation. After her mother's death, Dickinson described in a letter the survivor's "existence" as "homeless at home," but that phrase also seems to describe a more general disenfranchisement, the curious homelessness, of one tightly embedded in the paternal home where the power of the Word of the Father was built into the roof and walls that defined consciousness.

For Dickinson's whole career and for H.D. in *Trilogy*, the undeniable preeminence of the Word of the Father and the relative absence of a maternal, discursive power replicate the plotline of what Margaret Homans has called the "story of language." This story is echoed in many founding texts of our culture, from Genesis to psychoanalysis, and describes the significance of language in our phallocentric culture as predicated upon an absent referent identified with an absent, literal mater.[17] In asserting that the circumstances of Dickinson's and H.D.'s historical homes dovetail with the preeminence of the Word of the Father in their discursive homes in the canonical literary tradition, I am not claiming that Dickinson's genius derives from her "fall" into language from being denied in infancy sufficient preverbal language play by her mother.[18] Nor do I agree with Freud that H.D.'s "dangerous symptom," her mystical vision or her lesbianism, represents a search for her lost mother.[19] Rather, I am asserting that as writers, each of them had to realize that their discursive home, the origin of their printed "I," is in what Luce Irigaray calls in *This Sex Which Is Not One* the "economy of the same," the dominant language that tautologically both asserts the Word of the Father and reflects its power. This fact makes the vision and authority, the "eye" and "I" of each poet, "homesick": sickened or destabilized by the conditions of their linguistic homes and nostalgic for what is absent, a story of origins in which the female, discursive "I" is legitimated by the presence of a Word of the Mother.

For both poets, this inherited story of language manifests itself in their work in dramatizations or performances of the power of the paternal Word. While Dickinson takes comfort in the belief of her dead loved ones that they were indeed "going home" by "going to Heaven," she declares, "I'm glad I don't believe it / For it would stop my breath—" (79). Personifying paternal power as "Burglar, Banker, Father" similarly leads to a confession of her own powerlessness: "I am poor once more" (49). Loss of breath and poverty here imply not only physical death or destitution, but poetic silencing or emptiness as the poem itself slows and stops on the internal rhyme of "poor" and "more." The combination of poverty and breathlessness recurs in another poem where the rush of ambition similarly falters on a consideration of consequences. In poem 172, the "poverty" of failure is balanced by the ecstatic anticipation of "so much joy!" and by the example of others as "poor" as the speaker who have "ventured all upon a throw!" and "gained!" Reveling in an excess of language, the speaker's reasoning gallops forward: "Life is but Life! and Death but Death! / Bliss is but Bliss, and Breath but Breath!"

The speaker's ecstasy falters, not when turning to possibility of defeat, for it "means nothing *but* defeat," but when she considers the attainment of her goal, her "Heaven":

> repeat it slow!
> For Heaven is a different thing,
> Conjectured, and waked sudden in—
> And might extinguish me! (172)

The bouncing, regular rhythm of the poem's earlier lines is disoriented here as the speaker's voice figures the possibility of its own extinction. Dickinson's masterful manipulation of meter here shows how the dramatization of heaven's power or that of the "Burglar, Banker, Father" was simultaneously a performance of her own discursive power. Applying this idea to Dickinson's general prosody suggests that her famously eccentric dashes that pepper the page with such graphic urgency—slicing, stopping, and remaking the basic hymn meter that informs her verse—are a way of forcing the rhythms associated with the Word of the Father to conform to idiosyncratic patterns of her own breath.

A similar dynamic of dramatizing the power of the Word of the Father in a performance spotlighting the power of her own word informs H.D.'s work but is inflected differently by the layering of her representation of the Word of the Father with her engagement of the first sons of her generation, the male inheritors of paternal tradition like Ezra Pound, Richard Aldington, and D. H. Lawrence. Unlike Dickinson, whose genius was representative not of her age but of the next, the different stages of H.D.'s poetry parallel the evolution of modernism. Though Pound influenced her early work, even inventing the signature "H.D. Imagiste," which came to mark her place in canonical literary history, H.D.'s "crystalline" poems represent the principles of imagism more strongly than any of its other proponents' works. The tendency of mainstream literary history to read H.D.'s work mainly through Pound's label, "H.D. Imagiste," ignores her participation in the mythmaking projects of late modernism and her remapping of the cultural-textual intersections inherent in T. S. Eliot's "ideal order." As Susan Stanford Friedman notes, H.D.'s work is central to modernist mythmaking, though her "system" is "more religious than Williams or Pound, more esoteric than Eliot, and more syncretist than Yeats."[20] Even though *Trilogy* represents her most biblically focused performance of the Word of the Father, its blending of Christian with Egyptian and Greek mythology signals H.D.'s insistence on the common ground among these ancient traditions in shaping modern symbolic hierarchies. In *Trilogy*, H.D. dramatizes the power of the Word of the Father while simultaneously forging an authority in her own image. Later we will examine the significance of the Lady who bears the "unwritten volume of the new," but first we should note that here lies a fundamental difference in H.D.'s and Dickinson's revisionist strategies, one that offers a range of options to later revisionists.

H.D. draws parallels among biblical and other mythologies to evoke an alternative feminine bearer of the Word, while Dickinson engineers the "wiles of words" predominately within the biblical tradition to destabilize the significance of Logos and, in some cases, to offer the alternative of her own word. H.D.'s method depends primarily on analogy and metaphor while Dickinson's depends primarily on persona. This is not to say that H.D.'s method is multiple while Dickinson's is unified. Rather, H.D.'s range and juxtaposition of mythologies create an "alchemy"—an opening up of the process of making meaning— that Dickinson achieves though the multiple and contradictory postures of her persona toward the Word of the Father. Both strategies of metaphor and persona provide lines of revision that later revisionists employ in their own renegotiations of the "ideal order," the covenant with the dominant culture discussed in the introduction to this book.

Three personae characterize Dickinson's shifting postures in her dialogue with the Word of the Father. A voice confessing its own vulnerability, which earlier we saw dramatizing the power of the paternal Word, often assumes a childlike persona. Another voice assumes the persona of an outraged inquisitor, a defiant voice rejecting the paternal Word. Yet a third persona appears as a supremely poised intellectual voice that claims an equal authority over the Word, "this loved philology" (1651). The childlike posture occurs most commonly in Dickinson's earlier poems. Consider the "little girl" who hopes "the Father in the skies" will "lift" her just as she is, "Old fashioned—naughty—everything— / Over the stile of 'Pearl' " (70). This childlike voice also often confesses the inadequacy of its own power, authority, or vision. Awed by her recognition of "larger" problems with "statelier sums" than her own homework or accounting, the speaker of another early poem "files away" her "figures." Underscoring her sense of a lack of authority, this speaker concludes by addressing her own hand: "Wherefore, my baffled fingers / Thy perplexity?" (69). These same fingers find the ostensible "escape" of poetry to be another prison and "tug childish at my bars," "only to fail again" (40). This persona presents its authority, its "I," only as supplicant, seeking protection or pardon from the Word of the Father.

> Fold a tiny courtier
> In thine Ermine, Sir.
> There to rest revering
> Till the pageant by,
> I can murmur broken,
> Master, It was I— (151)

Dickinson's defiant "I" that appears in early and late works, by contrast, comes to being through outrage at the silence, the inaccessibility, of the "King" or master who "does not speak."[21] To Higginson, Dickinson complained that her family addressed "an Eclipse every morning—whom they call their 'Father.' "[22] The promise of divine explanation "when Time is over" offers no balm for the pain that Dickinson's emphatic repetition will not consign to silence, the "Anguish / That scalds me now—that scalds me now!" (193). Undaunted by the threat of "perjury," this "I" refuses "to pray / 'Father thy will be done' today / For my will goes the other way" (103). Quoting the Word of the Father to deny it as home of origin, Dickinson insists that she does not know the " 'Many Mansions,' by 'his Father' . . . snugly built" (127). Similarly, "Eden—the ancient Homestead" is just the setting for a bitter "sermon" from an "antique volume— / Written by faded Men" (1545). Yet even while this defiant voice criticizes God's treatment of Moses as a juvenile assertion of masculine dominance—"As boy—should deal with lesser Boy— / To prove ability"—the defiance melts to sympathetic identification with that biblical patriarch: "Old Man on Nebo! Late as this— / My justice bleeds—for Thee!" (597).

This impassioned critique of the Word of the Father that calls forth Dickinson's own sense of justice leads to the third persona that calmly reflects on her struggle with the divine pater in poems that themselves assume a posture of equality with the Word of the Father. Chronicling the alternation of submissive and defiant postures, Dickinson's most powerful "I" flirts with the promised peace of a biblical homeplace.

> He was weak, and I was strong—then—
> So He let me lead him in—
> I was weak, and He was strong then—
> So I let him lead me—Home. (190)

However, as the use of off-rhymes in this first stanza between "then" and "in" and "strong" and "home" suggests, there is no ultimate resolution. Thus, the poem concludes with an emphatic denial of closure in this dialogue with divinity: "He strove—and I strove—too / We didn't do it—tho'!" Similarly, playing upon "host" as symbol of homely hospitality and of communion with Christ, Dickinson reflects upon the ebb and flow of her dialogue with the Word of the Father: "He was my host—he was my guest . . . So infinite our intercourse / So intimate, indeed" (1721). The infinite and equal character of this dialogue fosters Dickinson's most radical poetics that destabilize the Logos of biblical tradition, making an outright bid to "steal the language."[23] Before we turn to moments in Dickinson's and H.D.'s work where the poets "steal home," however, we should first examine H.D.'s strategies of analogy and metaphor that function like E.D.'s personae to loosen the grip of biblical tradition on ontologies of home.

The sacred power of the biblical Word of the Father was analogous for H.D. to the masculine-dominated authority of the secular discourse of psychoanalysis. Both biblical tradition and psychoanalysis represent masculine-identified systems that H.D. studied and modified. As Friedman has argued, the poetic alchemy that H.D. performs on Christian tradition in *Trilogy* parallels her earlier engagement of psychoanalysis in her therapy with Freud. Particularly pertinent is the fact that both traditions represent influential ontological narratives, since the oedipal situation has functioned in the twentieth century as another Genesis, a story of the origins of human identity, gender, and possibilities for authority. Moreover, H.D. used the figures from the Bible in her work with Freud, identifying him as Moses and identifying the symbol of Bethlehem, the biblical site of Christ's nativity, with her own family origin. Conversely, the figures and methodology of psychoanalysis provide a basis for H.D.'s revision of Scripture in *Trilogy*, particularly in her exploration of dream imagery.[24] The analogy that H.D. drew between these two discourses allowed her to use her reflections on her relationship with Freud to work through the same problem reflected in Emily Dickinson's shifting personae: the daughter's problematic lack of authority in the power hierarchy implicit in biblical tradition. We might even see the discourse of psychoanalysis operating as a focal point for the process of transference, which allows H.D. to work through the gender bias of biblical tradition and represent it differently in *Trilogy*. Supporting this hypothesis are the facts of *Trilogy*'s composition: the three sections of this long work were written after her therapy helped to resolve a writing block and were coterminous with her composition of a memoir titled *Tribute to Freud*.

The submissive, defiant, and equal postures assumed by Dickinson's personae also appear in H.D.'s negotiations with the Word; however, this drama of power struggle is not visible in *Trilogy* because it has taken place offstage, as it were. Both *Tribute* and "The Master," H.D.'s poetic account of her relationship with Freud, record a reckoning with the Word of the Father that enables the presentation in *Trilogy* of a spiritual vision of the Word of the Mother. The authoritative voice of this major articulation of H.D.'s biblical revision is notably free from agon with the Word of the Father. In this respect, *Trilogy* is remarkable not only in the history of biblical revision, but in the larger history of women's literature. It is not that H.D. is uninfluenced by the presence of the Word of the Father, the Western literary canon; it is rather that by inviting it into her own imagination, her poem, her authority, she names it, and thus creates a work that is simultaneously about its textual history and unfettered by that history.

The first section of "The Master" reflects H.D.'s submissive posture in her negotiation with the Word of the Father in that, like the title of her prose memoir of Freud, it too pays "tribute," an obligatory debt of one less powerful to the great.[25] The words of this father contained "measureless truth," and his "command was final."[26] Interestingly, this poem that begins by paying homage to Freud as semidivine wise man concludes twelve sections later with the assertion of another god, "that Lord become woman" (461). Like *Tribute*, "The Master," while lighting an appropriate candle or two before Freud's altar, actually illuminates H.D.'s authority. The second section immediately presents her motive for therapy, an investigation of her bisexuality: "I had two loves separate; / God . . . told the old man / to explain / the impossible, / which he did" (453).

Although asserting the helpfulness of Freud's diagnosis, H.D. simultaneously and defiantly revises it in both *Tribute* and "The Master." The calm assertion in the memoir that they "never argued" about the "greater transcendental issues" but "there was an argument implicit in our very bones" (13) appears in the poem as an argument that lasts "till daybreak" as the speaker confesses, "I was angry with the old man / with his talk of the man-strength" (455). Though she is only a student, H.D. asserts in *Tribute* that "the professor was not always right" (18). Though he will be remembered and "temples" founded "in his name," she asserts in "The Master" that only she, among all his clients and disciples, "will escape" this idolatry (458). Freud himself recognized in her disagreement with him that she was not a "disciple," to "heal / or seal / documents in [his] name" (458). Instead, the rift between their views, like Dickinson's defiance and outrage at the Word of the Father, ultimately fosters a regeneration of the poet's word.

H.D. claims Freud freed her "to prophesy" by declaring that " 'you are a poet' " (458). This authorizing of vocation links the three texts—*Tribute*, "The Master," and *Trilogy*—in the outcome of her negotiation of an equal authority with Freud's word, symbolized by her reworking of the vision of a feminine figure, which Freud read as a "dangerous symptom," into the heart of *Trilogy*. In the next section, we will examine the significance of the figure of the Lady in H.D.'s long poem, but now let us look at a related figure in both *Tribute* and "The Master," as a sort of first draft of the Lady who is so vital to *Trilogy*. In the prose memoir, H.D. recounts a discussion with Freud about his favorite statue, that of Pallas Athene, which was extraordinarily well preserved except for a missing spear. H.D. turns over Freud's description, "she is perfect," examining his several angles of appreciation. This bronze goddess is a perfect specimen of the work of her age and is perfectly preserved; appreciating her value, moreover, represents a bond between Freud and H.D. (70). Yet, in "The Master," H.D. reappraises both the figure's value and the value of Freud's teaching: her anger with Freud's emphasis on "the man-strength" in her own work precipitates an epiphany:

> I could not accept from wisdom
> what love taught,
> *woman is perfect.* (455)

Stanzas V, XI, and XII go on to depict a goddess who "conjures the hills" (456). Freud's figurine of spearless Pallas Athene or Nike appears in the poem as "Aphrodite," a "Rhodocleia" who "needs no man" because she contains "the dart and pulse of the male" (456). In between hymns to this "Lord become woman" are sandwiched several stanzas that return to the issue of Freud's legacy. The central placement of his naming of H.D.— " 'you are a poet' "—in stanza VIII underscores the centrality of that commission to the concluding representation of lesbian eros and the goddess:

> we were together
> we were one;
> sun-worshippers,
> we flung
> as one voice
> our cry
> Rhodocleia. (460–461)

This poem that begins as homage to Freud ends as praise-song to feminine eros and spirituality; thus, the final phrase, "that Lord become woman," reflects the transformative movement of the whole poem.

This movement from the master's discourse, the Word of the Father, to a word signifying the feminine is the enabling (pre)text to the vision of the divine Lady in *Trilogy*. The section describing her appearance draws primarily on the Bible and traditional iconography of the Virgin. However, it not only revisits Bethlehem (H.D.'s hometown and the site of the Gospels' key story of origins), but also "steals home" in its revision of the Virgin's significance. After listing the familiar ways of depicting the Virgin in stanzas 29 and 30, H.D. insists they cannot describe her vision, which she names "Our Lady of the Snow" (96). Here we see "that Lord become woman" once again as she is literally dressed in the attributes of Christ. Wearing the sign of Christ's cleansing powers, this Lady's veils "were *white as snow, / so as no fuller on earth / can white them*" (97). The italicization of this phrase from the Gospels (Mark 9.3), marks H.D.'s theft of biblical language. This "emphasis added" also marks this image as what Mikhail Bakhtin would call a "hybrid construction," a double-voiced discourse that in this case refers to both the Word of the Father and to H.D.'s word.[27] The Lady ultimately functions, however, to bear the poet's word.

This shift in authority is symbolized in the difference between traditional iconography of the Virgin and H.D.'s Lady. The famous marker of the Virgin's identity, the divine baby she commonly holds on her lap, is "not with her" (97). Instead, like many images of the Annunciation in Renaissance art, she carries "a book" (100). In this depiction of the Virgin, however, H.D. revises her usual relation to the Word. In Botticelli's *Annunciation*, for example, the Virgin looks up from her reading of the Bible, possibly from passages foretelling her own role in the Messiah's birth, to confront the angel and her destiny of bearing the Word, giving birth to the embodiment of Logos. The word that H.D.'s Lady bears, however, is not "the tome of the ancient wisdom," but "the blank pages / of the unwritten volume of the new" (103). While this Word at this moment is "unwritten," we learn that "its pages will reveal / a tale of a Fisherman" and of "jars" (105), precisely the tale that is the next section of *Trilogy*, "The Flowering of the Rod."[28] So, the Word of H.D.'s virgin signifies not only the Logos of the Gospels, but also the ontological story of her own word, which will conclude *Trilogy*.

While H.D. metaphorizes the process of "stealing home" in the figure of the Word-bearing Lady, Dickinson relies less on metaphor but employs a similarly self-referential poetics. The tendency of Dickinson's language to destabilize the process of signification and celebrate its own medium explains why some critics describe her work as protomodernist. Joanne Feit Diehl recognizes that through the "indeterminacy of language," Dickinson constructs "a radically modern linguistic home."[29] Just as H.D. supposes that the Lady blesses her reworking of ancient myths, her refusal to "forgo" her "heritage," her "birthright" as a writer, Dickinson too renames the "larceny" of her verse as "legacy" (7). Language is both the object and the medium of this inheritance.[30]

Claiming mortal participation in the divine Logos, Dickinson asserts that "the brain is just the weight of God" but shifts the crux of the comparison from the material realm of gravity to the discursive realm of sound: "they will differ—if they do— / As Syllable from Sound" (632). Hence, the syllable articulated in language is akin to the divine Logos. Similarly, the "fleshless chant" of a spiritualized nature offers "tufts of Tune / Permitted" only to "Gods, and me." This poem suggests that the poet's appropriations of divine music are a birthright, not so much stolen as realized.

> Inheritance, it is, to us—
> Beyond the Art to Earn—
> Beyond the trait to take away
> By Robber, since the Gain
> Is gotten not of fingers—
> And inner than the bone—
> Hid golden, for the whole of Days. (321)

So, "inner than the bone," inheritance is always an internal property, not an external "Gain." Reading this poem in conjunction with poem 1651 suggests, furthermore, that inheritance is internal not only to human subjectivity, but also to the field of discourse. Though not gotten "of fingers," inheritance is "Hid golden" in language.

Though "A Word made Flesh" seems to be a rare and monumentous occasion, only "seldom / and tremblingly partook," Dickinson wonders if we have not all "tasted" it. After all, "a Word that breathes distinctly" is immortal like "He / 'Made Flesh and dwelt among us.' " Like H.D.'s italicization, Dickinson's quoting of a description of Christ from the Gospels marks the dual reference of the phrase, as it points back to the Word of the Father even in its new incarnation in Dickinson's word. Dickinson, unlike H.D., never offers a feminine figure of the divine to bear another Logos,[31] yet the figure of poetry itself seems to perform that function in the poem's conclusion:

> Could condescension be
> Like this consent of Language
> This loved Philology. (1651)

Critics have read these lines as an audacious reversal of the more commonplace assertion of poetry as a trope for communion. Here, the mystery of transubstantiation is merely a trope for poetic making. As Homans has said of Dickinson's general revisionist strategy: "she proposes a revision in the entire structure of patriarchal religion, to the effect that the incarnation might become more like her poetry, instead of poetry aspiring to resemble the incarnation."[32]

Offering the "loved Philology" of her own word as at least an equal counter to the Word of the Father, Dickinson opens up the field of feminist biblical revision as a literary pursuit, as a way to remake a literary point of origin through modernist techniques of ambivalence and exploitations of language's self-referentiality (rather than through work grounded more centrally in the disciplines of history or theology, for example). Similarly, H.D.'s rewriting of a key ontological figure, the Virgin, as a bearer of her own word establishes a methodology and theme later writers will draw upon. The concluding two sections of this chapter will consider the ways that Dickinson's and H.D.'s appropriations of the authority of the Word of the Father are particularly inflected both by the impact of war and by their construction of audience.

The "Bodiless Campaign": Biblical Revision, Authority, and War

The importance of war in the biblical revision of both Dickinson and H.D. offers clues to explain the striking recurrence of war, both as subject and trope, in twentieth-century feminist biblical revision. First, there is the fact of the historical frequency of war: from the Civil War to Vietnam, every generation of American writers has lived through a time of war or its aftermath. It is only reasonable that World War I and II, profoundly important to twentieth-century history and to literary modernism, would also shape alternative currents in literary history. In addition to the historical impact of war is the significance of the discourse of war in the founding texts of the Western literary tradition. The biblical Word of the Father examined in the last section has been closely linked to the tradition of "arms and the man": the King James Version of the Bible, for example, was commonly taught side by side with *The Iliad* and other classic war epics. When Dickinson writes "There is a word / which bears a sword," she refers to the Bible, or rather, to the use of biblical rhetoric in war; but that line also points to the role of the literary tradition in "bearing" war—in recording and transmitting the discourse of war.[33]

Another tie connecting war to authority for women writers is the link between war and the representational matrix examined earlier in this chapter, "the woman question." Nineteenth-century gender ideology reflects the tradition of representing women as opposed to war due to their role as nurturers; some even claimed that women's suffrage would end war. The rhetoric and reality of suffrage, however, reveals a more complex relationship among women, representation, and war. British suffragettes readily cast their struggle as a war, and during World War I, the battle between the sexes became partially subsumed by the war effort. Reflecting this shift, the magazine *The Suffragette* was even renamed *The Britannia* in 1915.[34] Clearly, the failure of suffrage, of women's political representation, to prevent war particularly pressured women's literary representation. As Sandra Gilbert and Susan Gubar have shown, representations of women in male-authored texts during and after World War I tend to blame women for encouraging or benefiting from the sacrifice of men on the battlefield.[35] The real opportunities that opened up for women in England and America during World War I and II also broadened the scope of experience about which women could write. In *Three Guineas*, Virginia Woolf concludes that the best contribution women can make toward the protection of "culture and intellectual liberty" from the tyranny of war is "reading and writing in their own tongue" more earnestly than they have ever done before.[36] In short, Woolf offers the pen, borne by women, as a weapon against arms, borne by men. A later essay by Woolf, composed during the bombing of London, returns to this idea and sheds some light on what is at stake in the relation of gender, representation, and war both for a writer like Dickinson, who uses war primarily as a trope, and for a writer like H.D., whose *Trilogy* was inspired by and aimed at the war that shadowed its composition between 1941 and 1944.

In "Thoughts on Peace in an Air Raid," Woolf points out: "Arms are not given to the Englishwoman either to fight the enemy or defend herself. She must lie weaponless tonight."[37] Rather than support the war machine by producing the materials of war, Woolf urges women to fashion new ideas to help "the young Englishman . . . defeat the enemy." Echoing William Blake, who vowed never "to cease from mental fight," Woolf urges women to think and write "against the current, not with it."[38] H.D.'s therapy with Freud originated in precisely this kind of intellectual resistance. As Europe moved toward World War II in the 1930s, H.D. wanted to "stop drifting" with her generation "before the current of inevitable events swept me right into the mainstream and so on to the cataract." H.D. saw stepping back from the "current" of current events as a chance to "take stock" of what she "owns" before the disaster of another war.[39] As her statement implies, the crisis of war urged an examination of identity and power—in short, of authority. Soon we will examine how H.D.'s authority in the biblical revision of *Trilogy* answers the crisis of war, but first let us briefly examine how Dickinson's authority reflects the structure implied in Woolf's command to women writers not to "cease from mental fight."

More poems written by Dickinson just before, during, and after the Civil War refer, either directly or indirectly, to that conflict than is generally assumed.[40] Though Dickinson only rarely mentions a particular episode or the death of an acquaintance, several poems seem to comment on the use of Christian rhetoric in justifications of war (readily apparent, for instance, in the well-known hymn "Onward Christian Soldiers" and in Julia Ward Howe's Civil War poem, "The Battle Hymn of the Republic"). In an early poem, after three stanzas evoking the romantic idiom of battle, Dickinson mocks the emperor's attempt to take stock of the victory: "How many *Bullets* bearest? / Hast Thou the Royal Scar?" The inventory of battle recorded on the soldier's body ironically represents both the success of the battle and the loss of his life: "Angels! Write 'Promoted' / On this Soldier's brow!" (73). In such poems, Dickinson's critique seems doubly directed at both popular uses of Scripture to make the war acceptable to the general population and to the prominence of war rhetoric in the ancient text itself.[41]

War appears most forcefully in Dickinson's work, however, not as the bodily struggle of men on the field, but as the "bodiless campaign" of souls on the discursive field of language:

> The Battle fought between the Soul
> And No Man—is the One
> Of all the Battles prevalent—
> By far the Greater One. (594)

This posture of spiritual and poetic agon is often represented by the defiant voice that, as discussed in the last section, challenges the Word of the Father. As critics have noted, "wrestling," particularly the biblical scene of Jacob's wrestling with the angel for divine blessing, characterizes a whole line of thought in Dickinson's work.[42]

This literary stance of agon with the Word of the Father posits a clash of two wills, two authorities, and, as we saw in "A Word Made Flesh," Dickinson sometimes declares her own word victorious. The danger of taking on "Heaven," however, is that it also "might extinguish" the poet's voice. Whatever the outcome, the poet's authority in this situation is always constructed through opposition. This fact is tremendously important to the twentieth-century poets who follow Dickinson, like Sylvia Plath and Anne Sexton. Though Dickinson's biblically informed poetry is varied, containing multiple postures as we have seen, it is always a one-on-one "mental fight" with the divine pater. Her oscillation between apostasy and submission inaugurates a line in biblical revision of simultaneously expressed desire and anxiety. The linguistic ambiguity of poems like "A Word Made Flesh," which locate the poet's victory or alternative to Logos in the discursive realm, foreshadow the "fiercely defiant voices of modernist literary experimentation."[43] And in the unresolvable clash of "He strove and I strove too," the seeds of the perpetually crossed forces of modernist sous-ratour are evident.[44]

As we discovered in the last section, H.D.'s battle with the Word of the Father takes place "offstage" from the drama of *Trilogy*, and she operates not through one-on-one opposition, but through a comparison (and sometimes a collapse) of Christian, Greek, and Egyptian mythologies, of biblical and psychoanalytical stories of origin. The primary trope for the poetics of her biblical revision, then, is not linguistic war but linguistic "alchemy." Without World War II, however, the alchemy of *Trilogy* would not have come into being.

In a letter written shortly after finishing *Trilogy*, H.D. explains that the "great good lady" of that poem is Venus, who "is shining now full and splendid out of my bedroom window—or into it. As we still have black-out, this is good for seeing stars."[45] Just as the ban on the use of lights during the war allowed H.D. to better observe the evening sky, so the crisis itself created a kind of imaginative blackout that brought into stark relief H.D.'s own authority and clarified the symbolic history of the stars. Adalaide Morris has established how the progress of the war for H.D. was both backdrop and spur to the composition of *Trilogy*.[46] The gathering of the power of the poet in the first section, "The Walls Do Not Fall," is an arming for Woolf's "mental fight," written during the aggressions of 1942, when "Evil was active in the land" and the "Dev-ill" was "tricked up like Jehovah" (5). The redeeming vision of the Lady in the second section, "Tribute to the Angels," was composed during what H.D. called "a wonderful pause" in the war, just before D day of that same year.[47] And the hope of the nativity in the concluding section, "The Flowering of the Rod," written just before Christmas 1944, was a gesture of faith in spite of the apparent eminence of victory by Adolf Hitler before the Battle of the Bulge.[48]

The rush of women and the civilian population in general to produce material support for the war made many question the abstract, immaterial support offered by writers, as impractical or even effeminate. The doubting "you" of "The Walls Do Not Fall" accuses "poets" of being "useless," even "pathetic," echoing an assertion from a letter that infuriated H.D. that writing poetry was a "pathetic" activity during war.[49] H.D.'s authority in *Trilogy* rises in direct opposition to this view and attacks the image of the useless poet by claiming the legacy of biblical Logos: "remember, O Sword, / you are the . . . latter-born / . . . *in the beginning / was the Word*" (17). Yet crucial to *Trilogy*'s project is also an awareness of the role of poets, of literature, in creating a discourse of war that feeds the making of actual wars.[50] Thus, the biblical legacy H.D. claims (and its ties to the other founding texts of Western civilization) represent both her authority and her responsibility for that heritage.

H.D. admits her hand is implicated in the work of war: "Without thought, invention," without "the Word's mediation," the "Sword" "would have remained / unmanifest in the dim dimension" (18).

Recognizing this responsibility leads H.D. to attempt in this long poem, originally titled *War Trilogy*, to exploit the visionary aspect of her inheritance to change the relationship between the Word and war.[51] In this respect, H.D.'s biblical revision is not only a literary and personal project, but an overt, self-conscious cultural project. Like the other long poems of late modernism, which confronted the disaster of war-ravaged Europe with the antidote of a "rag-bag of civilization," H.D. would "rather drown remembering" (121). Remembering, however, was for H.D. quite a different thing from Pound's and Eliot's search for the "missing contents" of modernism.[52] Instead of embarking on a nostalgic search for the past Word of the Father, H.D. attempts to reassemble and reconstruct, and thus re-member, a mythological history that would foster the birth of a different culture, rather than a resurrection of the dead, patriarchal one.[53]

The sign that precipitates the different ontological story of the "The Flowering of the Rod," the tree charred by bombing, evokes a key symbol of that dead, patriarchal history even as it dramatizes its dying and H.D.'s transformative resurrection of it. When the poet is "prepared for burial,"

> she set a charred tree before us,
> burnt and stricken to the heart;
> was it may-tree or apple? (82)

"She" here is the goddess Astoroth and/or H.D.'s muse, and the tree evokes simultaneously the "rood," the wooden cross of Christ's crucifixion, and the infamous apple tree of Genesis. As the sound play between "burial" and "apple" suggests, Eve's first eating of that forbidden fruit of knowledge is tied to mortality and all the pain that has plagued humanity since the fall.

But as that image recurs, the "burnt-out wood crumbling" in the "old garden square," we find the apple tree, only "half-burnt out," miraculously "blossoming" in the rubble (84–87). This "flowering of the wood," like the Christian paradox of Christ's death, is a sign of life. Centering this image on an apple tree, however, collapses this sign of redemption with the sign of original sin and thus brings Eve's act into dialogue with Christ's. In the celebration of the flowering apple tree is an implicit reevaluation of Eve's sin as salvational. Disobeying the Law of the Father to eat the fruit of the tree of knowledge is also, interestingly enough, a figure for H.D.'s poetic project here, which consumes the fruit of other trees, of Greek and Egyptian mythologies. In short, legitimating Eve's sin (by merging it with Christ's sacrifice) justifies H.D.'s own sin, her heresy in the central image of the second section, the removal of the Christ child from the Lady's arms and the substitution of her own book.

Rewriting the plots of the New Testament, H.D. in the final section of *Trilogy* draws on mythologies older than Christianity to create a version of the gospel that might support a future without war. Just as the worshippers of Rhodocleia refuse to say "pity us," so the voice of "The Flowering of the Rod" rejects pity, the sign of Golgotha, the sacrifice of Christ: "With no thought of duty or pity," she turns to what she loves and seeks home, or inheritance, there. Although the "harvester" of culture, of time, prepares to reap war and death in Europe in 1944, H.D. insists that "this is not our field":

> we have not sown this:
> pitiless, pitiless, let us leave
> The-place-of-the-skull
> to those who have fashioned it. (115)

In the final section of *Trilogy*, H.D.'s earlier turning away from the "grave-edge" to articulate another "heritage" in her vision of the Lady culminates in a revision of the pietà. To understand why this image is a focal point for the tensions of war and gender, one must see the interrelation of two analogies. As representations of the pietà are to the institution of maternity, so representations of Golgotha, or the crucifixion, are to the institution of war.[54] The pietàs that present Mary holding on her lap a son full grown and already wounded by his sacrifice capture the slippage between the icon of the Madonna and child and the crucifixion. More broadly, though, soldiering and mothering have been traditionally conceived as the opposed vocations of each gender. As Susan Schweik demonstrates through her readings of the popular contemporary poetry of World War II, the pietà and the nativity were often evoked as comforting countersigns to war. H.D., however, "destabilizes" the poetic staple of the "stable" scene by underlining the relation between Christian imagery to what Michel Foucault calls the production of "docile" bodies that are so necessary for war.[55] Freeing Christ from the "junk-shop / paint-and-plaster medieval jumble / of pain-worship and death-symbol" and Mary from the traditional split between the two Marys of the Gospels, virgin and whore, disrupts the function of this ontological story in regulating gendered behavior (27).

By presenting the vision of the multifold image of the goddess through Kaspar, a wise man, H.D. brings these ancient traditions before the eyes of any reader who would imagine the nativity. Playing on the long tradition of woman's hair as eroticized symbolic textile or text, the loosening of Mary Magdalene's hair reveals to Kaspar the crowned "lady" (150) and the traditions of "Paradise / before Eve" (155), which she represents—Venus, Astoroth, even Lilith—all mingled as "daemons" (157) or presiding spirits of this holy image of feminine divinity. This vision articulates another ontological story, a feminine divine always "before Adam," "before Eve" (154–155). The presence of the Magi's gift of myrrh, symbolic of a transcendental life force, then, is already a part of Mary, who H.D. has shown in "Tribute to the Angels" participating in the ancient goddess tradition: the word most bitter "marah"

becomes "mar," "mere," "mater," "Maia," and "Mary, / Star of
the Sea, Mother" (71). The poem's conclusion underscores the
revision in this pietà and its implications for the relation of war
and gender. The fragrance of "all flowering things together"

> . . . came from the bundle of myrrh
> she held in her arms.
>
> London
> December 18–31, 1944. (172)

Signing this poem with place and date—bombed-out London as
a victory by Hitler is threatened—places this pietà overtly in the
context of war while disrupting the traditional representation of
the relationship between the pietà and war. In sum, the "bundle
of myrrh" in Mary's "arms" symbolizes the kind of armament
that whole poem produces for a Blakean "mental fight."

In this cultural function of *Trilogy* lies another difference between H.D.'s and Dickinson's work as models for later revisionists. While Dickinson's wrestling with the Word of the
Father may expand how a reader understands the possibilities
for authority in our culture, the reader learns this only through
eavesdropping on Dickinson's very personal and individual dialogue. *Trilogy*, by contrast, is designed as cultural therapy, and
the audience is an integral part of its design.

"Write, Comrade, Write!": Audience and Authority

Where my Hands are cut, Her fingers will be found inside—
—Emily Dickinson
(quoted in Martha Nell Smith's *Rowing in Eden*)

Without someone warm and breathing on the other side of the
page, letters are worthless.
—Virginia Woolf, *Three Guineas*

These two remarks by Dickinson and Woolf reflect the shaping power of specific "warm and breathing" audiences on the biblical revision of both Dickinson and H.D. As Martha Nell Smith has argued, the focus of critical attention on Dickinson's male mentors and friends has obscured the influence on her work of her correspondence with women, particularly her long and intimate relationship with Sue Gilbert, her sister-in-law.[56] While more scholarship on H.D. has considered the importance of her ties to other women, the moment when Pound titled her "H.D. Imagiste" has functioned as sort of literary ontological story. As a counter "birth" scene to H.D.'s authority, particularly for her appropriation of the biblical Word of the Father, I look instead to the moment in 1920 when H.D.'s lover, Bryher (Winifred Ellerman), witnesses H.D.'s vision, the "writing on the wall" at Corfu, and urges her to "Go on." Both Bryher and Sue Gilbert's roles as tangible female audiences facilitated H.D.'s and Dickinson's productions of biblical revision. While all biblical revision implicitly posits a textual audience in the Word of the Father, Dickinson's and H.D.'s examples suggest that this "talking back" is also shaped or articulated toward another audience, the "warm and breathing" textual presences of their female friends and mentors. It seems likely that this audience has a dual function in biblical revision: it offers a counter or opposing female presence to the Word of the Father and simultaneously functions as a metonym, or representational stand-in, for the larger audience of possible readers.

There is a good deal of evidence that Dickinson's relationship with her sister-in-law substantially influenced her poetry. Although the energy of Dickinson's early plea in a letter to Gilbert—"write, comrade, write!"—was sometimes negatively charged over the twenty-five years of their friendship,[57] the fact that Sue received over two hundred poems suggests that Emily was writing to and/or for Sue.[58] The only known substantial revision Dickinson made for a reader was the drafting of an entirely new second verse to "Safe in their alabaster chambers," with hopes that "this verse would / Please you better—Sue— / Emily."[59] Furthermore, as Smith has shown, Dickinson playfully appropriates and subverts biblical language in letters to Sue to both express and justify the intensity of her feelings for Sue.[60] While Dickinson often claims a "satanic" or "wicked" identity[61] that forfeits any claims on a heavenly home, she was unwilling to surrender Sue.

> To own a Susan of my own
> Is of itself a Bliss—
> Whatever Realm I forfeit, Lord,
> Continue me in this! (1401)

The "Realm" of Susan is symbolized in Dickinson's poetry as "Eden," as Smith has argued, and that idyllic realm is the sign of both Dickinson's passion for Sue and her territory for imaginative creation.[62]

As the tangible audience of Dickinson's poems, Sue functioned as an alternative inspiration and audience to the absent, omnipotent Father whom Dickinson so often addressed. "Owning" a Susan, furthermore, represents a textual claim, since Dickinson so often figures "Susie" in her poems, either directly, as in the poem quoted above, or indirectly, as in the Eden poems. This textualized "Sue" offers another kind of counter to the Word of the Father in that she supplements the tradition of her nineteenth-century women precursors whom Dickinson read so enthusiastically.[63] As a representation of women's textual authority, the textualized "Sue" belongs with the figure of Charlotte Brontë in Dickinson's elegy and the portrait of Elizabeth Barrett Browning that hung in Dickinson's bedroom.[64]

H.D.'s relationship to Bryher is analogous to Dickinson's relationship to Sue Gilbert in that erotic feeling was closely associated with "creative power" in both.[65] H.D.'s recollection in *Tribute to Freud* of Bryher's presence and support during her vision of Nike and other symbols at Corfu in 1920 documents

H.D.'s understanding of Bryher's significance to the vision that later inspires biblical revision of figures of a feminine divine in *Trilogy*. Bryher's encouragement and later participation in this vision seems to be integral to H.D.'s rejection of Freud's diagnosis of it as a "dangerous symptom" and her eventual reading of it as "inspiration."[66] As the "writing on the wall" appears to H.D., she asks Bryher if she should "break away," but Bryher replies "without hesitation" that she should "Go on."[67] Bryher's support of this fantastical episode is here implicitly juxtaposed to Freud's diagnosis of it as a "symptom" of illness. The significant thing is not that this recollection of events paints Bryher as good or faithful mentor and Freud as bad or doubtful mentor; after all, later in this same memoir, H.D. calls Freud "midwife to the soul."[68] However, it is crucial that in H.D.'s mind in 1944, just as *Trilogy* was being completed, Bryher functioned as a counter to Freud. H.D. insists in *Tribute* that the "extraordinarily gifted and charming people" she has known, such as Freud, Pound, and Aldington, one assumes, could not have "shared" this vision; "only the girl who stood so bravely there beside" her could witness it. H.D. admits that "without her," she "could not have gone on" and asserts that Bryher even apprehends the final image when H.D. cannot continue.[69]

In sum, reevaluating this "dangerous symptom" in *Tribute* and "The Master" becomes a textual stepping-stone to the celebrations of the figures of the feminine divine in *Trilogy*. Each of these representations (Nike in *Tribute*, Rhodocleia in "The Master," and the Lady in her many forms in *Trilogy*) possesses a common source in what H.D. calls "the writing on the wall" vision facilitated by the "warm and breathing" audience of Bryher. In her focus on myrrh in *Trilogy*, furthermore, H.D. may even offer another tribute, not to Freud, but to Bryher. The open-voweled sound of "myrhh" suggests a link to the similar ending sound of H.D.'s companion's rather unusual pseudonym. In a poem celebrating words as "boxes / conditioned to hatch butterflies," could not "myhrr" be a partial cryptogram for "bryher"? The constellation of "m," "y," "h," and two "r"s is unusual in English, and the transformation of the "b" in "bryher" to the "m" in "myrrh" possibly could represent meta-morphosis.

Like Emily's Sue, H.D.'s Bryher served as audience for the greater part of her life and work, despite periods of tension or separation. To conclude this chapter, I would like to suggest how the function of these "warm and breathing" audiences on Dickinson's and H.D.'s biblical revision relates to the reception of that work by larger audiences. H.D.'s reevaluation and cele-bration of women's erotic capacity and power in the three re-lated texts examined here was an intrinsic part of the function of her work as "cultural therapy." As Morris has demonstrated, H.D.'s "visions" both position her "outside of history" in their transcendent aspect and endow her work "with a public power and presence" within history.[70] The roles of generational spokeswoman, therapist, and prophet collide in the construc-tion of H.D.'s authority in *Trilogy*. Thus, her relationship with Bryher shapes the issues and underscores the urgency of the work she offers to the larger audience.[71] Although Dickinson may not have been writing for immediate or wide publication, her relationship with Gilbert also effects the reception of her work. The intensity of what I will call the "other-directedness" of Dickinson's poetry creates a kind of rhetorical excess that flavors the reader's experience of the text. Dickinson's writing for Sue is a sort of counter to her one-on-one game with the Word of the Father. That layered dialogue is so charged, so ex-cessive, that it emits a kind of emotional energy that readers re-spond to, often feeling as if they have entered into a relationship with the author herself. This explains the strange fact that critics have noted concerning the diversity of readers who identify with Dickinson and the extremity of their convic-tion that they truly know the author.[72] In other words, I am suggesting that it is Dickinson's "owning" of a "Susan of [her] own" that makes so many readers feel as if they own an Emily of their own. Thus, Dickinson's biblical revision also may even-tually accomplish another kind of cultural work, though it is not characterized by the same sense of cultural mission that marks *Trilogy*.

It is the personal and profoundly ambivalent battle with the Word of the Father that Plath and Sexton inherit from Dickinson, as the next chapter will demonstrate. For the confessionalists, the paternal authority of the text remained strong. Coupled with the individual agon in confessional poetry, however, are strategies also reminiscent of H.D.'s biblical revision. Two cornerstones of H.D.'s biblical revision resurface in Plath's work in particular: the strategic collage of mythologies and the focus on the Virgin. Although Plath was profoundly influenced by the masculine literary canon, the biblical revision of both of these feminine precursors provides a crucial interpretive framework for a reading of the search for a Word of the Mother in Plath's and Sexton's poetry.

Notes

1. All parenthetical references to Dickinson's poems in the text correspond to the number of the poem in Thomas H. Johnson's *The Complete Poems of Emily Dickinson* (Boston: Little, Brown, 1960).

2. H.D., *Trilogy* (New York: New Directions Books, 1973), 6. Hereafter, all poetry quotations from *Trilogy* are cited parenthetically by stanza number in the text and refer to page numbers.

3. Joanne Feit Diehl, *Women Poets and the American Sublime* (Bloomington: Indiana University Press, 1990).

4. See Larry Ceplair, ed., *The Public Years of Sarah and Angelina Grimke: Selected Writings (1835–1839)* (New York: Columbia University Press, 1989); Karen Sanchez-Eppler, *Touching Liberty: Abolition, Feminism, and the Politics of the Body* (Berkeley: University of California Press, 1993); and my article " 'A System of Complicated Crimes': The (Con)Fusion of Subjects in Angelina Grimke's Public Speeches," *Women's Studies* 27 (1997): 31–52.

5. G. C. Baldwin, *Representative Women: From Eve, the Wife of the First, to Mary, the Mother of the Second Adam* (New York: Shelson, Blakeman, and Co., 1856), vii.

6. Ibid., 24.

7. Quoted in Martha Nell Smith, *Rowing in Eden: Rereading Emily Dickinson* (Austin: University of Texas Press, 1992), 5.

8. Margaret Homans, *Women Writers and Poetic Identity: Dorothy Wordsworth, Emily Bronte, and Emily Dickinson* (Princeton, N.J.: Princeton University Press, 1980), 215.

9. Cynthia Griffin Wolff, *Emily Dickinson* (Reading, Mass.: Addison-Wesley, 1988), 3–35.

10. H.D., *Tribute to Freud* (New York: New Directions Books, 1974), 32.

11. See Barbara Guest's biography of H.D. for a discussion of her Moravian heritage: *Herself Defined: H.D. the Poet and Her World* (New York: Doubleday, 1984), 9–25.

12. Wolff, *Dickinson*, 50.

13. Ibid., 118–122.

14. Quoted in ibid., 45.

15. Ibid., 61–62.

16. See Guest's description of H.D.'s mother in *Herself Defined*, 17.

17. Margaret Homans, *Bearing the Word: Language and Female Experience in Nineteenth-Century Women's Writing* (Chicago: University of Chicago Press, 1986), 4–13.

18. Wolff makes this argument about Dickinson's "fall into language" (*Dickinson*, 36–65).

19. H.D., *Tribute*, 17, 41.

20. Susan Stanford Freidman, *Psyche Reborn: The Emergence of H.D.* (Bloomington: Indiana University Press, 1981), 209–210.

21. Wolff sees Dickinson's attacks as an attempt to "wound" the divine Father as she has been wounded by his absence (*Dickinson*, 159).

22. Quoted in Wolff, *Dickinson*, 148.

23. See Alicia Ostriker, *Stealing the Language: The Emergence of Women's Poetry in America* (Boston: Beacon Press, 1986).

24. Freidman, *Psyche Reborn*, 223.

25. As Alicia Ostriker notes in "What Do Women (Poets) Want?: H.D. and Marianne Moore as Poetic Ancestresses" (*Contemporary Literature* 27, no. 4 [1986]: 475–492), H.D. is punning with the title of her memoir (p. 488).

26. H.D., *Collected Poems, 1912–1944*, ed. Louis L. Martz (New York: New Directions Books, 1983), 451. Hereafter, H.D.'s poems from this volume are cited parenthetically by page number in the text.

27. See Nancy Miller's discussion of the need to read women's writing with special emphases in "Emphasis Added: Plots and Possibilities in Women's Fiction" (in *Subject to Change: Reading Feminist Writing* [New York: Columbia University Press, 1988]), and Mikhail Bakhtin's discussion of hybrid constructions in Michael Holquist's edited collection *The Dialogic Imagination: Four Essays* (Austin: University of Texas Press, 1981), 304.

28. Albert Gelphi also makes this connection in "Re-membering the Mother: A Re-reading of H.D.'s *Trilogy*," in *Signet: Reading H.D.*, ed. Susan Stanford Friedman and Rachel Blau Duplessis (Madison: University of Wisconsin Press, 1990), 330.

29. Joanne Feit Diehl, " 'Ransom in a Voice': Language as Defense in Dickinson's Poetry," in *American Women Poets*, ed. Harold Bloom (New York: Chelsea House, 1986), 23–39. Also see Wolff's biography, *Dickinson*, 151.

30. See Ostriker's general argument in *Stealing the Language*.

31. Dickinson's celebrations of nature offer the closest thing in her work to a delineation of a particularly female figure of the divine, as she consumes a "sacrament of summer days" or vows to remain true to the mountains, her "strong madonnas."

32. Homans, *Women Writers and Poetic Identity*, 214.

33. *Arms and the Woman*, edited by Helen M. Cooper, Adrienne Auslander Munich, and Susan Miller Squier (Chapel Hill: University of North Carolina Press, 1989), particularly foregrounds the constitution of war in discourse.

34. James Logenbach, "The Women and Men of 1914," in *Arms and the Woman*, ed. Cooper, Munich, and Squier, 97–123.

35. Sandra Gilbert, "Soldier's Heart: Literary Men, Literary Women, and the Great War," in Sandra Gilbert and Susan Gubar, *No Man's Land: The Place of the Woman Writer in the Twentieth Century*, 2 vols. (New Haven, Conn.: Yale University Press, 1988), vol. 2, 258–323.

36. Virgina Woolf, *Three Guineas* (New York: Harcourt Brace Jovanovich, 1938), 89.

37. Virgina Woolf, "Thoughts on Peace in an Air Raid," in *Death of the Moth and Other Essays* (New York: Harcourt Brace Jovanovich, 1942), 243.

38. Ibid., 244.

39. H.D., *Tribute*, 13.

40. See Shira Wolosky, *Emily Dickinson: A Voice of War* (New Haven, Conn.: Yale University Press, 1984).

41. See Wolosky on Dickinson's response to the use of the Christian paradigm of life through death in the war rhetoric of her day (ibid., 66–68).

42. See Wolff's *Dickinson*, 151–159.

43. See Diehl's " 'Ransom in a Voice,' " 38.

44. On that modernist clash, see Marianne Dekoven's *Rich and Strange: Gender, History, and Modernism* (Princeton, N.J.: Princeton University Press, 1991).

45. Quoted in Freidman, *Psyche Reborn*, 249.

46. Adalaide Morris, "Signaling: Feminism, Politics, and Mysticism in H.D.'s War Trilogy," *Sagetrieb* 9, no. 3 (1990): 121–133.

47. Quoted in ibid., 128–129.

48. Ibid., 133.

49. Ibid., 123.

50. See Susan Schweik, *A Gulf So Deeply Cut: American Women Poets and the Second World War* (Madison: University of Wisconsin Press, 1991).

51. Morris notes that *Trilogy* was originally titled *War Trilogy* ("Signaling," 121).

52. See Ellen Friedman, "Where Are the Missing Contents?: (Post)Modernism, Gender, and the Canon," *PMLA* 108, no. 2 (1993): 240–252.

53. Melody M. Zajdel argues that *Trilogy* also rewrites some of the other major works of modernism, seeing, for example, in H.D.'s transforming sibyl a counterfigure to negative feminine figures (the siren and the tawdry sibyl) that contribute to the misogynist vision of cultural decay in Eliot's "Waste Land": " 'I See Her Differently': H.D.'s *Trilogy* as a Feminist Response to Masculine Modernism," *Sagetrieb* 5, no. 1 (1986): 7–16.

54. Schweik, *A Gulf So Deeply Cut*, 261.

55. On the "stable," see ibid., 266. Foucault asserts in *Discipline and Punish* (New York: Vintage, 1977) that a "docile body" is that which "may be subjected, used, transformed, and improved" (p. 136).

56. For the epigraph to this section, see Smith's *Rowing in Eden* (148). Dickinson "self-published," in the alternative medium of her correspondence, three times as many poems to women than men, and Sue was by far the greatest single recipient (Smith, 131). The fact that

Dickinson's brother, Austin, and his mistress, Mabel Loomis Todd, censored many references to Sue in Dickinson's letters and poems as they prepared them for publication indicates their anxiousness to suppress something about Dickinson's feelings for Sue.

57. See Betsy Erkkila's reading of the class dynamics and other sources of strain in Dickinson's relationship with Gilbert and other women in *The Wicked Sisters: Women Poets, Literary History, and Discord* (New York: Oxford University Press, 1992).

58. Smith, *Rowing in Eden*, 170.

59. Quoted in ibid., 193.

60. Ibid., 160–168.

61. See Erkkila, *Wicked Sisters*, 23.

62. Smith, *Rowing in Eden*, 205.

63. See Erkkila, *Wicked Sisters*, 60–84, and Cheryl Walker, *The Nightengale's Burden: Women Poets and American Culture Before 1900* (Bloomington: Indiana University Press, 1982), 107–109.

64. See Walker's description of Barrett Browning's picture (*Nightengale's Burden*, 107).

65. Smith, *Rowing in Eden*, 131.

66. H.D., *Tribute*, 47.

67. Ibid.

68. Ibid., 116.

69. Ibid., 48–56.

70. Morris, "Signaling," 129.

71. Indeed, *Trilogy* is very aware of its audience, figuring both rationalist detractors and sympathetic readers, "companions of the flame," in the "you"s it evokes. For a discussion of how the poem builds audience into its own structure, see Alicia Ostriker's "No Rules of Procedure: The Open Poetics of H.D.," in *Signet*, ed. Friedman and Duplessis, 348, and Freidman, *Psyche Reborn*, 213–214.

72. Wolff, *Three Guineas*, 3–10.

Chapter Two

"Much Madness Is Divinest Sense": The Biblical Revision of Anne Sexton and Sylvia Plath

A Rhetoric of Confession

In the fall of 1958, Anne Sexton and Sylvia Plath met in a poetry workshop run by Robert Lowell at Boston University. Though Lowell's 1959 collection, *Life Studies,* is credited with beginning the confessional movement, it is the work of his two women students that has become practically synonymous with confessionalism. The critical backlash against this American poetic movement that dared to place personal experience, particularly anguishing experience, at center stage has thus disproportionately targeted Sexton and Plath and has contributed to a general lack of appreciation of the range and cultural significance of their poetry. Though Sexton's later poetry is often understood as religious while Plath's is not, this chapter investigates how both poets undertake a larger project of cultural revision though their very different dialogues with the Bible. This generation's argument with the Word of the Father necessarily rises out of the confessional movement. Just as H.D.'s biblical imagination was rooted in modernism, so these later poets' biblical imagination was "born," as Sexton says, "doing reference work in sin / and born confessing it."[1] Some of Sexton and Plath's confessions, like their male contemporaries', relate to their mental illnesses, but in each case "Much Madness," as Dickinson said, leads indeed to "divinest sense," or at least to serious attempts to make sense of divinity.

The implications of the confessional movement for biblical revision are twofold. First, the rhetorical nature of confessionalism—always a speaker's address to an audience—places the woman writer's "I" firmly in the foreground and spotlights her "signature." While Dickinson's unmistakable "I" governs her dialogue with the Word of the Father, the "I" that reappears in American women's poetry roughly a century later is both her daughter and a thoroughly postmodern character. Sexton's and Plath's speakers, far from being raw representations of the author (as mischaracterizations of confessionalism sometimes suggest), range from autobiographic performance artists to mythic personae. A closer examination of the tangled issue of reference in Plath's poetry will illustrate the complexity of the confessional speaker.

To understand Plath's biblical revision, one must first understand how it functions within the complicated and sometimes chaotic universe of her heteroglossia. Just as the mingling of Christian with Egyptian and Greek mythology fuels H.D.'s revision in *Trilogy*, so the collapse of ancient traditions and modern discourses fuels Plath's biblical revision. To clarify the issue of reference in Plath's work (and, in particular, the reference to biblical texts), two seemingly contradictory aspects of her use of language must be understood. First, her poetry is fundamentally discursive, systematic, and self-referential. Yet, it has the effect of disrupting and opening the discourses it engages. What I term the "discursive nature" of Plath's work derives from the uncommon degree to which her poetry engages other narratives. As her poem "Words" suggests, the axe of her word makes the wood of literary tradition "ring" as it sends transformative "echoes traveling / off from the center."[2]

In contrast to those who interpret the poetry as primarily autobiographical, I maintain that one cannot assume that Plath's poems necessarily refer to biography or to anything outside of language. I offer this not as a truth about all language, but merely as a description of Plath's writing. This is an important caveat to an examination of biblical themes because the Bible is often assumed to be a platform to launch meditations on an atemporal, ahistoric, and prelinguistic reality. On one hand, Judith Kroll's hypothesis that Plath would have explored the religious and mystical themes of some of her late work had she lived longer seems to be supported by a poem like "Mystic," which asks: "Once one has seen God, what is the remedy?" (268).[3] However, many of Plath's poems written in the fall of 1962 seem to evoke not an atemporal supreme being, but the history of representations of biblical narrative. Consider the difference between the question asked in "Mystic" and the one asked in "Winter Trees": "Who are these pietàs?" (258).

A strange convergence in the scholarship on Plath's work suggests that its unusually discursive nature creates a kind of textual opacity or sense of limit. Despite differences in theoretical approaches and political agendas, diverse critics describe a similar sense of fixity. Kroll's sense in 1976 that there is no "temporal movement" or "development" in the poetry because the mythology of the white goddess determines meaning may be related to Jahan Ramazari's contention in 1993 that Plath's elegiac poems are trapped by melancholic mourning. Similarly, James Young's view that Plath's use of Holocaust tropes may have stalled her imagination parallels Alicia Ostriker's view that the polarized rhetoric of poems like "Daddy" ultimately reinscribes the power relations it critiques.[4] This sense of boundary or limit in her work reflects both the drive of modernist poets to weave the "monuments of unaging intellect" of literary history into their works and the questions raised by postmodernists about the self-referential nature of language.

If the "I" of Plath's poetry is a "shifting world of words," and if her voice is "an intertextual space in which her web of obsessions" defines "itself in relation to the institution of literature," then the most significant reference of Plath's language is to other bits of her language and, indeed, to whole literary traditions and cultural discourses.[5] For example, the figure of an ascending woman in "Lady Lazarus" signifies intertextually with all the late poems that conclude with her ascent, just as the recurring figure of a descending or departed pater intertextually links the poems in which he appears, such as "Full Fathom Five," "The Colossus," and "Daddy." Both of these figures, furthermore, take their meanings from the tropes of literary and biblical traditions through which Plath articulates them.

Though this embeddedness in other narratives creates the sense of an almost closed textual world, the explosive energy of Plath's poetry tends to open the discourses she engages. In fact, the multiplicity and density of references to other narratives suggest that biography is just one of many intertexts. The kinetic energy and revolutionary American impulse for which critics have praised the late work may be as attributable to the variety and juxtapositions of discourses (such as psychoanalysis; Christian, Greek, and Egyptian mythology; Holocaust imagery; and 1950s domestic ideology) as to the controversial "confessional" subject matter.[6] These Plathological combinations of discourses and excessive loading of signification overdetermine the autobiographic reference of any one image or poem. In short, the "life" that was Dickinson's "loaded gun" has been fired by Plath's hand.

A priest once advised Sexton that God resided in her typewriter, but that might be even more true for Plath.[7] It is not just that the kingdom of heaven exists within her heart, but that God, in Plath's work at least, may be a typographical event, a sign referring to another sign, rather than to an atemporal referent. For Sexton, by contrast, the typewriter was but a conduit, a path for the poet who could not "walk an inch without walking to God" (472). Sexton's biblically informed poetry is characterized by a more familiar search for meaning, for a great, omniscient divine figure who she hopes exists outside of history, outside of time. Ironically, though, for Sexton, this figure who is outside history is always inside herstory—the plot of her own personal family romance.

Though her spiritual search is more directly mapped against autobiography, Sexton's speaking "I" is no more simply autobiographic than Plath's. Diana Hume George has isolated four different stands of reference for Sexton's "I" in her confessional poems.[8] While Plath's poetry is complicated by her rampant heteroglossia, the energy of Sexton's biblical revision derives from its performative nature. Nowhere is this general pattern revealed more clearly than in her dramatic monologues and explorations of mythic personae in "The Jesus Papers."

At the end of this sequence of poems, which reimagines key events of Jesus' life as moments of oedipal crisis, comes the self-reflexively titled "The Author of the Jesus Papers Speaks." After the speaker claims the origin of some of the sequence's most disturbing imagery "[i]n my dream," she relates God's command that "we must all eat sacrifices. / We must all eat beautiful women" (345). Here, Sexton forces the reader's awareness of our consumption of her performance, in this case, her performance of her dream of the Gospels. Sexton's *Complete Poems* brim with such "seductive" moments that tear down "the invisible veil" between author and audience even as she makes us aware of the pretense of our separateness, of our disconnectedness.[9] A fashion model in her youth, Sexton was very aware of her striking presence on and off the page. Her passion for performance drove her decade-long work on her own play, *Mercy Street*, and packed her readings throughout the 1960s and early 1970s. Diane Middlebrook, her biographer, even argues that the most appropriate category for Sexton may be that of the performance artist.[10] The fundamentally dramatic, performative nature of Sexton's speaking "I" raises two related questions: What exactly does it perform, and for whom?

These questions lead to my second point about the implications of the confessional movement for biblical revision. We have just seen how the rhetorical nature of confession—as a speaker's address to an audience—inflects the woman writer's

"signature," but it also inflects its audience; that is, it poten-
tially shapes its hearers. The way Sexton's conclusion to "The
Jesus Papers" compels her audience to take responsibility for
our consumption of "beautiful women" perfectly illustrates this
function of confession. After all, this poetic movement takes its
name from the Catholic sacrament that cleanses the soul and
opens up a space for forgiveness, acceptance, and, most importantly, change.

In one sense, of course, this is nothing new for poetry; Ralph
Waldo Emerson defines the authentic American poet as the
one with a "new confession" for a "new age."[11] The middle
decades of the twentieth century, however, had perhaps more
to confess than other ages. America was coming to terms with
the aftermath of two world wars: particularly, the horrors of
the Holocaust, the changing articulation of gender, and the
struggle for racial equality in the developing civil rights movement. Robert Lowell's treatment of his experience as a conscientious objector, for example, illustrates how the intensely
personal cargo of confessional poetry inevitably is freighted
with cultural significance. Since Anne Sexton's and Sylvia
Plath's confessions focus more on their experience of femaleness—their lives as daughters, lovers, wives, and mothers in a
prefeminist culture—many readers overlook the political and
cultural dimensions of their work. Diana Hume George, however, correctly describes Sexton as "a poetic analyst of her culture."[12] In this respect, biblical revision in the confessional era
continued its "cultural work," much as H.D.'s meditation on
the role of the poet during World War II peformed a kind of
cultural function, as we saw in the last chapter. The rhetorical
triangle basic to biblical revision remains a useful way to con-
ceptualize the poets' address to both the ancient text and to
their contemporary culture. The speaking "I" occupies the top
of the triangle, and its confession simultaneously addresses
both its textual precursor, the Bible, and its human audience
(particular readers and the larger culture). The reading of Sexton's biblical revision that follows is relatively brief because of

the excellent criticism that already exists on the subject. Almost nothing has been said, however, about Plath and the Bible; so this chapter focuses on her at greater length and then concludes with a consideration of the impact of both authors' intimate audiences on their biblical confessions.

"Mrs. Sexton Went Out Looking for the Gods": The Biblical Revision of Anne Sexton

The Death Notebooks, Sexton's seventh book of poetry, published in 1974, the year of her suicide, opens with "Gods," a poem that sardonically surveys the spiritual quest that reaches back to her earliest volumes and concludes with the posthumous book *The Awful Rowing to God*.

> Mrs. Sexton went out looking for the gods.
> She began looking in the sky—
> expecting a large white angel with a blue crotch.
>
> No one.
>
> She looked next in all the learned books
> and the print spat back at her.
>
> No one.
>
> She made a pilgrimage to the great poet
> and he belched in her face.
>
> No one.
>
> She prayed in all the churches of the world
> and learned a great deal about culture.
>
> No one.
>
> She went to the Atlantic, the Pacific, for surely God . . .
> No one.
>
> She went to the Buddha, the Brahma, the Pyramids
> and found immense postcards.

No one.

Then she journeyed back to her own house
and the gods of the world were shut in the lavatory.

At last!
she cried out,
and locked the door. (349)

Her taped voice reading this poem reiterates "No one" with a
deep-toned solemnity that counters the flip, irreverent diction
of her search for the "gods."[13] What her performance of this
poem makes clear is that her spiritual need was serious but that
humor was always a tool, a drug in a sense, that made that un-
filled need bearable. Unlike Plath, she found no sustaining images in "learned books" or in non-Western mythological and
religious traditions. Like H.D., however, she did find in the
narratives of Freudian psychology ways for making sense of her
need. "Gods" begins by lampooning a desexualized spiritual
imagination that would drape the angels' crotches in virginal
blue and ends by humorously locating the source of all religious quests in the "lavatory," the space that is so crucial in
Freudian thought to children's development of individual identities, sexuality, and creativity.

The importance of psychoanalysis to Sexton's poetry cannot
be overstated. She began writing at twenty-eight, when, after
several suicide attempts, her doctor encouraged her to write
about her experience to benefit others struggling with mental
illness. She was delighted to discover "at the nuthouse," as she
said, people who "talked language."[14] Finding a community
that valued figurative language spurred Sexton's creativity, and
the language of psychology itself—association, transference,
displacement—became essential to her understanding of her
work. As we will soon see, the male modernists represented
one poetic ideal for Plath. Sexton's "people," her poetic lineage, included her contemporaries who also wrote about their
mental problems, like John Berryman and W. D. Snodgrass,

and classic poets of extremes, like Arthur Rimbaud.[15] Though she read widely and received honorary degrees after winning the Pulitzer Prize, Sexton's formal education extended only through high school. She learned sonnet structure by watching I. A. Richards, a New Critic, lecture on public television.[16] Without the poet's usual grounding in literary tradition, the narratives of psychoanalysis became her path to an identity as a writer.

While her mental breakdown and efforts at recovery dominate her first book, *To Bedlam and Part Way Back* (1960), the desire for relief from suffering is intertwined with a desire for spiritual belief in *All My Pretty Ones* (1962) and continues throughout her career. Sincere belief in Christianity appears as something that belongs only to others: for instance, her biblically named friend Ruth in "With Mercy for the Greedy" (62–63) and her mother in "The Division of the Parts" (42–46). Though she cherishes the cross Ruth sent, it is like her recently dead mother's possessions: her "part" is offered to her, but she cannot claim her inheritance. Sorting though her mother's belongings and her own discomfort with the rituals of mourning, she feels radically inauthentic, even fraudulent:

> I imitate
> a memory of belief
> that I do not own. I trip
> over your death and Jesus, my stranger
> floats up over my Christian home, wearing his straight
> thorn tree. I have cast my lot
> and am one third thief
> of you. (42–46)

The poem closes Sexton's first volume with the image of the poet as supplicant as she prays for her mother to "make" her an inheritor. The balm of faith, however, is only one "part" of the inheritance she craves. Spiritual belief is bound up with writerly power. The speaker realizes she is performing another ritual of resurrection, bringing her "old love" "flapping back" with her "rhyming words." It is not Christ's redemption, after all, that she needs, but the inheritance "without praise / or paradise" of the "Lady of my first words."

In the interim between her first and second books, that prayer appears to have been answered. When in "With Mercy for the Greedy" she regretfully declines her friend's call to make "the Sacrament of Confession," she offers her own poetic confession as substitute. As Middlebrook argues, Sexton's metaphors are "vehicles for the spirit" and perform much the same function as traditional religious rituals.[17] These two early poems also point to a gendered complication in Sexton's poetic entanglement of spiritual power and writerly authority. The women, Ruth and her mother, possess a traditional faith she cannot own: "need is not quite belief," as the speaker admits to Ruth. Poems in *All My Pretty Ones* and *Live or Die* (1966) suggest, furthermore, that the need for a maternal blessing of her words never quite equals belief either.

Most of Sexton's poems that engage biblical figures and themes feature male speakers. A telling exception is "For the Year of the Insane" (131–133), a prayer to the Virgin Mary. In "the domain of silence," "the kingdom of the crazy and the sleeper," the speaker's "hands" cannot write but "are alive" only on their rosary. Though Mary, like the healing Christ of the Gospels, appears as a "tender physician," she cannot heal the supplicant's crisis of articulation. This "little mother" seems even less likely to grant verbal power than the "Lady of my first words." The "domain of silence," of waiting, after all, is Mary's realm, and the poem ends in despair, with the speaker complaining that her mind is "locked in the wrong house."

This overview of Sexton's early biblically informed poetry illustrates how it assumes the familiar "story of language" that was discussed in the introduction. As Margaret Homans has shown, this master plot of culture, which assigns the feminine to the inarticulate or preverbal realm, underwrites Freudian narratives of human development as well as more ancient stories of origin, like Genesis.[18] The Logos or creative power of a Father God dovetails readily in Sexton's mythopoeic world with the sexual power of the father in the family romance. Sexton's revisionary biblical poems manifest her desire to get out of the "wrong house" of the silent, feminine realm and to get into a masculine structure of signification. Looking back to "The Division of Parts," even as the speaker disavows belief, she identifies as a "thief" with Christ, who was crucified with thieves. In her second volume, the speaker assumes the persona of Christ to face the consumption by rodents of his body that will keep "the miracle" of his resurrection alive ("In the Deep Museum," 64–65). The third volume, *Live or Die*, which also offers her painful prayer to Mary, confesses in "Consorting with Angels" (111–112) to being "tired of the gender of things" and demonstrates her desire to transcend gender altogether, as the speaker declares, "I'm no more a woman / than Christ was a man." Whether one sees this disavowal of gender as a heroic bid for universalism or as the self-loathing of the oppressed, it ironically was the path for Sexton into her critique of "the gender of things" in biblical myth and the "story of language."

Sexton squarely addresses that story and the silencing of the mother in "The Legend of the One-Eyed Man" (112–115). Her work with psychoanalysis inspires this oedipal reading of Judas's betrayal of Christ. The poem concludes that because of a "dream" of Judas's mother,

> he was altogether managed by fate
> and thus he raped her.
> As a crime we hear little of this.
> Also he sold his God. (115)

As Hume George suggests, this ending shocks because "the speaker trivializes the crime we have regarded as most heinous—the betrayal of God—in favor of the ones against the feminine that our culture has itself trivialized."[19] The combination of this critique with Sexton's mastery of revisionary sto-

rytelling in *Transformations* (1971), her uncanny retelling of
Grimm's tales, lays the groundwork for her reimagination of
the Gospels in "The Jesus Papers" (337–345) in *The Book of
Folly* (1972).[20]

In "Jesus Suckles," Christ evolves from blissful union with
his mother to a toddler's self-assertion and need to "run everything" and to "own," especially his mother. Ostriker deftly illustrates how Sexton's imagination of Christ's infantile
development critiques the place of the feminine in culture. As
he grows, Jesus enters "the dualistic universe" posited by
Christianity and our larger culture, where the mother and the
flesh she represents must be rejected.[21] Similarly, "Jesus Un-
born" insists that the divine gaze that brought Christ to the
world is for Mary the "executioner's eyes" that "shuts her lifetime up."

The epigraph to this sequence of poems—"God is not
mocked except by believers"—points, like her verbal performance of "Gods," to the seriousness underlying Sexton's sardonic wit. In "The Legend of the One-Eyed Man," Judas notes
that the New Testament is "small" (only opening "Its mouth
. . . four times"), "out-of-date," and "somehow man-made."
Sexton opens the mouth of the New Testament once more,
writing, as it were, a Gospel According to Anne. Though many
Christians may see this sequence as blasphemous because of its
depiction of Jesus' desire for his mother and its deflation of his
performance of miracles, Sexton's imagination begins with the
orthodox assertion that Christ was also human. Her insight
into his reality can come only from her experience of her own
humanity; as noted earlier, the sequence concludes with the
confession that this is the author's dream of Jesus' life. Behind
Jesus' oedipal crisis, of course, is Sexton's. Once again, the spiritual and psychoanalytic are embedded in each other and express Sexton's evolving sense of authority. Her writerly oedipal
desire spurs her transgression. Rather than sleeping with the
Father, she imagines herself as the Son. Taking up the phallic
pen similarly transgresses gender boundaries to appropriate

the Father's power. It is only with this authority that "The Author of the Jesus Papers" can speak with God in the sequence's closing lines: once again, "we must all eat sacrifices. / We must all eat beautiful women." Performing as God, Sexton confesses that female sacrifice, the consumption of women, lies at the heart of the Bible and that we all have "eaten" this fact.

Though the place of the feminine in the Bible as it is traditionally interpreted is critiqued in "The Jesus Papers," no alternative, or even a call for change, is offered. Sexton's next book, however, *The Death Notebooks*, offers something different. No maternal or feminine divine takes center stage, but the speaker sheds the role of the Son in her evolving spiritual family romance to claim the role of sister in "O Ye Tounges" (396–413). She retains a strong identification with the male, however, by positing a twin identity. Sexton acknowledges her inspiration for this sequence of ten psalms by naming her twin brother "Christopher," after Christopher Smart, the eighteenth-century British poet famous for his combination of mysticism and madness. It is with this persona that Sexton offers the broadest, most hopeful representation of the divine of her whole career: a God "as large as a sunlamp" who may "laugh his heat at you." Though the divine is always male here, images of breasts, milk, mothers, and song recur and present the feminine with more power than in any of Sexton's other biblically informed poems.[22]

I think it no accident that this poem that celebrates, as Middlebrook has argued, the growth of the speaker's daughter into womanhood is also the only of Sexton's biblically informed poems to overtly appropriate biblical form.[23] Like Smart, Sexton plays with the form of the Psalms, writing long-lined, loosely rhymed verse that imitates the biblical Psalms, alternating sections beginning with "let" with ones beginning with "for." Just as "Anne and her daughter master the mountain," Sexton seems to feel comfortable working in the form of the ancient work. It must be admitted, though, that the sequence is uneven poetically. For all the calm power the speaker claims, stunning lines like "we swallow magic and deliver Anne" mingle with clumsy metaphors of "altitudes" that "plunge." The brilliantly bizarre "heaven of jelly rolls and babies laughing" collapses into the banal world of "Cannon towels." The faltering craft here underlines the fragility of the psychic world of the relatively empowered sister-speaker. In fact, in Sexton's next book, *The Awful Rowing to God*, her spiritual imagination returns to the metaphor of the archetypal family and focuses once again on the daughter's relationship to an all-powerful pater.

Though "The Rowing Endeth" (473–474) clearly hopes to offer a triumphant image, many readers are disappointed by the "imaginatively small and fraudulent God" that dominates the last poem.[24] After rowing to "the island called God," the speaker plays a poker game with God. Though she thinks at first to win with a "royal straight flush," he, of course, holds all the aces. God's laughter rolls into her "mouth" as "He doubles right over" her. Even the "Absurd laughs" as she closes the poem by professing her love for this "untameable," all-powerful force. Here at last is the image of the God that Mrs. Sexton went out looking in her poem "Gods." However, absence, with its solemn refrain of "No one," has become such an overwhelming presence that the speaker's declaration of love sounds like a "grotesque attempt to placate" the omnipotent God.[25]

The resolution of spiritual quest here seems inseparable from defeat in a power struggle; once again, the underlying issue may be the writer's sense of authority in the frame of the family romance. Hume George has shown how the island of God resembles Squirrel Island, home of Sexton's grandparents and her childhood vacation retreat. The great father here may reconfigure Sexton's own grandfather, who, significantly, was a professional writer. His name, Gray, was Sexton's own middle name and symbolizes writerly talent in her family mythology.[26] One cannot know if Sexton consciously connected this image of a powerful island God with her grandfather; in any event, she committed suicide after marking the galley proofs of *The Awful Rowing to God*.[27]

Reading the Bible through the psychoanalytic lens of the family romance equipped Sexton with a powerful gender critique, but it also seems to have fixed her imagination in an always-already powerless position. Psychoanalysis was also a catalyst to Plath's biblical imagination, though she used it not only to construct a critique of the place of the feminine in the "story of language," but also to imagine a feminine figure of the divine.

"The Girl Who Wanted to Be God": Sylvia Plath's Biblical Revision

I think I would like to call myself "The Girl who wanted to be God." Yet, if I were not in this body, where *would* I be—perhaps I am *destined* to be classified and qualified. But, oh, I cry out against it. I am I—I am powerful—but to what extent?
—Sylvia Plath, *Letters Home*[28]

Plath's mature work can be read as an attempt to answer this question, which she asked in a journal entry at age seventeen. To estimate the extent of one's power, however, requires a scale; as an award-winning student and Cambridge fellow, it was likely that Plath's main scale for self-measurement would be the canonical literary tradition. Journals and letters show that she weighed her accomplishments against those of established poets, "those god-eyed" ones and one of their chosen successors, her husband and fellow poet, Ted Hughes.[29]

Even this youthful journal entry reveals an awareness that the world's measuring instruments will find her lacking and classify and quantify her desire for omnipotence. The iteration of "I" nine times underlines the struggle and determination of the writer's self-assertion and foreshadows the faltering and reiterated "I"s of many of the "Ariel poems." Sandra Gilbert has shown how Plath's fear that this self-assertion would be circumscribed or contained is related to the gender of "this body," and she acutely connects Plath's premonition of frustrated ambition with her sense of "rivalry" with the great male authors of canonical literary tradition and her fear of becoming a "scribbling woman" or poetess.[30]

Several poems from Plath's juvenilia, written close to the time of the journal entry above, similarly demonstrate her desire for authority, disgust with the hyperfeminine figure of the poetess, and dread of some divine retribution for the audacity of "the Girl who wanted to be God." "Female Author" rehearses the misogynist stereotypes of the dilettante poetess who "nurses chocolate fancies" and "nibbles an occasional bonbon of sin" (301). This proper little sonnet evidences the author's awareness that the highest praise a woman poet could receive in the 1950s was that which Lowell eventually bestowed on Plath: she is "certainly not another poetess."[31] As Steven Gould Axelrod demonstrates, Plath's formal, classical education implicitly taught her that literature was a male preserve and that even the "language belonged to men."[32] The traditional sonnet form of this exercise, as well as the unflattering depiction of the woman writer, seems designed to win praise from an important representative of the male literary tradition, Plath's instructor at Smith College.[33] Letters written by the adult Plath also proclaim her pride in the unfeminine qualities of her verse, as validated by her personal representative of the masculine literary tradition, her husband, who was "very strictly disciplining . . . [her] work and study."[34]

This ambition to be a great "woman singer" also characterizes "Aerialist," another work from Plath's juvenilia that anticipates key issues and situations of her mature work.[35] Here a girl dreams of being an "adroit young lady" and performs feats of daring on the high wire only to be stalked by hostile forces that seek to "shatter to atoms" of her nine lives (331–332). This "outrageous nimble queen" may in fact be the object of the quest of the speaker of the late poem "Stings," who has "a self to recover, a queen" (215). This early poem, however, clearly shows ambivalence about quest and achievement. Like Sexton's declaration that "I say such and such / and heaven smashes my words" (472), Plath's dreaming girl wakes to face "penalty for her skill" and must "walk in dread" that the "whole / Elaborate scaffold of sky" will "fall" as a "racketing finale on her luck" (332).

Plath's poetry, journals, and letters all offer evidence that "the Girl who wanted to be God" felt herself an exile from literary heaven. Consider "Song of Eve," part of Plath's unpublished juvenilia, probably written during her undergraduate years at Smith. This twenty-four-line poem in rhymed couplets opens with Eve speaking "colored words" that create light and life. In the first stanza, her voice is all-powerful, usurping even God's role in pronouncing creation "good." But by the poem's final stanza, this song reclaims the traditional narrative of the fall, assuming complete blame for the fact that all "stories have a bitter end."[36] It is this mixture of ambition and ambivalence, of desire for authority and dread of punishment, that molds Plath's biblical revision into the sous-ratour or double-cross structure.[37] As martyr and rebel,[38] Plath could well approach the preserve of male authority with the hermeneutics of suspicion and desire that Ostriker has shown to be fundamental to feminist revision. Critics have suggested that these conflicted reactions to the literary tradition derive from Plath's conflicted feelings for her father. If "Daddy" is indeed "daddy-poetry," the indictment of the patriarchal figure as "bastard" not only masks the speaker's sense of illegitimacy,[39] it also depletes and obliterates the speaker's voice. The stasis and tendency toward self-cancellation that is implicit in sous-ratour is evidenced by the same poem. To borrow the words of "Death & Co.," while Daddy is "done for," "somebody" else is too: the speaker is "through."[40] Whether the biblical God is a trope for a mortal pater, or the mortal father a mold for the artist's imagination of an immortal deity, biblical Fathers and earthly Daddies seem thoroughly intertwined in Plath's poetic imagination, just as the two coalesced in the Word of the Father for Dickinson.

Another source of the limiting "classifications" feared by the "Girl who wanted to be God" may reside in the overlay of the plot of New Testament redemption for Plath on top of the poet's negotiation with literary fathers. The Christian narrative of salvation through self-sacrifice may well be a force influencing the speakers' disappearances. In other words, it is not language itself, but rather a particular discourse at a particular historical moment that presents problematic and ultimately disabling narrative structures.[41] Just as the confessional genre offered, as Kathleen Margaret Lant has shown, potent tropes for self-revelation but ultimately led Plath to reinscribe the canon's traditional misogyny, so the Gospels offer both useful and problematic literary structures. Though the poet's marginal and ambivalent relation to the masculine (and often misogynist) literary tradition does create the representational problems Lant describes, it may also simultaneously foster revisionist authority.[42] In sum, Plath's relationship to the male literary tradition was both oppressive and exclusionary, but not wholly or uniformly so.

Plath recognized that her husband, who was mentored by T. S. Eliot himself, was a "direct descendent" of the male modernists.[43] Lines like James Joyce's famous praise of "The Waste Land" for "ending the idea of poetry for ladies" indicate how the misogynist strain in modernism trivializes the aspirations of a woman poet. Yet Plath literally "mastered" the masters, receiving an M.A. from Cambridge and eventually literalizing her relation to the tradition by actually setting up residence in W. B. Yeats's former house. Despite the rebellion against paters that electrifies her late work, those very poems display important affinities with male modernists, although, like her modernist predecessor Ezra Pound, she sought to "carve" and reshape the stuff of her inheritance. My readings will trace her reweavings of several poetic threads from Eliot and Yeats, but here let me suggest some of the general or structural similarities of Plath's midcentury work with modernism.

While some of Plath's key works depend upon allusions to the classics of Western literature, from Greek and biblical myths to William Blake, Yeats, and Theodore Roethke, she—

taking a cue from Lowell and Sexton—reinvents modernism's "allusiveness" by broadening the scope of reference to include social discourses marked by the languages of domesticity, psychoanalysis, and Holocaust imagery. This weaving of social and literary voices is related to the second characteristic of modernism that Plath appropriates: the technique of mask and persona that aligns poems like "Lady Lazarus" with the dramatic monologues of "Hugh Selywn Mauberly" and "The Love Song of J. Alfred Prufrock."[44]

All of the techniques that Plath adopted from the modernists were also adapted by her in ways that reflect her marginal relation to that tradition. For example, Plath's classical allusiveness springs not only from her respect for the tradition, but also from her desire to wield its authority, to claim an inheritance. Unlike her modernist precursors, however, she did not offer the cornerstones of tradition as stays against contemporary social decay.[45] Like Dickinson's use of multiple personae, Plath's shifting allegiances destabilize the authority of the tradition and its constructions of gender. Plath's efforts to distance herself from the stereotypes of the poetess influence the kinds of masks she uses and her constructions of voice in the late poetry. The cool, observant detachment of the early exercise "Female Author" differs in style but not in strategic purpose from the outrageous ferocity of "Lady Lazarus" and "Purdah." Neither, certainly, presents "another poetess."

Plath's liminal position in relation to literary authority parallels her liminal position to biblical authority. Indeed, the two types of authority are often fused, with biblical Logos representing the ultimate literary authority. In a letter, Plath boasts about an exam essay she wrote at Cambridge, casting God as "the Supreme Stylizer."[46] While a later journal entry confesses to finding "great peace" in the "Book of Job," the author reaffirms her postlapsarian position and resolves to "read the Bible" for its "symbolic meaning, even though the belief in a moral God-centered universe is not there."[47] While these quotations demonstrate that the Bible was not a fount of spir-

itual authority for her, many of her journals and letters, as well
as her poetry, use biblical authority as a trope for literary authority. In a early journal entry, Plath casts herself as "one
mortal imperfect Eve with a fierce full rightness . . . corre-
sponding to the ecstasy experienced by the starving saint on
the desert." The occasion for Plath's donning of the persona
of Eve, and even giving it a prophetic spin, is nothing less than
her first "real professional acceptance" by *Harper's*.[48] To sum-
marize, these writings indicate that biblical authority functions as a sign representing literary authority and that Plath's
ability to trope on the Bible derives from her marginal relation
to both traditions. In other words, her biblical revision is possible precisely because she is an exile from the religious and
literary tradition. Similarly, her use of Holocaust imagery may
be possible only because of her nonmembership in the Jewish
community.[49]

Although some readers are offended by Plath's use of biblical
tropes, many more have criticized her use of images from the
Holocaust to represent other horrors, particularly gender violence. Irving Howe best represents the thrust of this critique
when he calls it "monstrous, utterly disproportionate, when
tangled emotions about one's father are deliberately compared
with the historical fate of the European Jews."[50] Similarly,
Marjorie Perloff objects to Plath's "forays into the 'larger
world': commenting on the Holocaust or on Christianity."[51] As
we have just seen, though, "tangled emotions" about father figures signify far beyond the facts of biography and effect the
very foundation of Plath's construction of literary authority. Interestingly enough, the poems that disturb readers because of
their use of Holocaust imagery, such as "Lady Lazarus" and
"Mary's Song," are also key poems of Plath's biblical revision.
The combination and interaction of tropes from the Bible and
tropes from the cultural narrative of Nazi atrocities seems to
result for some readers in "heresies of holocaust," to borrow a
phrase from Plath's juvenilia (326). Critics who object to Plath's
Holocaust references assume that the author is commenting on

or addressing the historical reality of the Holocaust. As we saw in the first section of this chapter, however, social reference in Plath's work is a vexed issue because it is inevitably entangled in her heteroglossia. The tongue that speaks of Auschwitz simultaneously evokes other referents. Plath is no more simply "commenting on" the Holocaust than she is simply commenting on gender oppression or the relationship of Christian tradition to the oppression of both women and Jews.

The iconography of the Holocaust, in fact, functions as a cultural text that Plath pilfers and shapes just as she does biblical texts. Evidence from journals, letters, and interviews shows that Plath conceived of the events of the Holocaust both as historical facts and as especially charged metaphors for oppression.[52] The Holocaust references are part of a larger network that foregrounds the "body" through an elaboration of what Gayle Wurst calls an "aesthetics of violence," which pits speakers against older "means of expression" in a process of "self-overcoming."[53]

The work that most critics regard as representative of Plath's mature voice is characterized by a continual quest to redefine the self. The question that concludes "Poppies in October"— "Oh my God, what am I" (240)—is the question that drives Plath's poetry from 1962 to 1963. Consider a chronological selection from statements of the speaker's struggle for self-definition:

> I am a great event ("Three Women," March 1962, 176)
>
> I am not a Caesar ("The Arrival of the Bee Box," October 4, 1962, 213)
>
> I'm through ("Daddy," October 12, 1962, 224)
>
>   I Am a pure acetylene Virgin
> ("Fever 103," October 20, 1962, 232)
>
>   I am the arrow
> ("Ariel," October 27, 1962, 239)

I am a miner ("Nick and the Candlestick," October 29, 1962, 241)

I am his ("Purdah," October 24, 1962, 243)

I am your opus . . . your valuable ("Lady Lazarus," October 23–29, 1962, 246)

O God, I am not like you ("Years," November 16, 1962, 255)

Even this brief selection of statements supports the critics' assertion that the central project of the late work is the construction of an authorial self through language.[54] The fact that many of these attempts to define the "I" occur in poems that contribute to Plath's biblical revision suggests that the revision of the speaker is intertwined with the revision of biblical tropes. The subject that emerges from Plath's interrogation of identity attempts to present an immortal, deific being more like the author's female self than like any masculine other. A quick look at Plath's Eve imagery will demonstrate that, like Dickinson, Plath asks, "Why am I not Eve?" The critical evolution of her use of biblical tropes over her career sets the stage for our final examination of the two main trajectories of Plath's revision that witness the birth of a new speaking subject, a female deity.

Adam and Eve in Plath's early work represent the original, archetypal couple that provides a model for the speaker's marriage.[55] Evidence from letters suggest that the Genesis narrative provided a frame for Plath's understanding of her experience; she describes her future husband shortly after their first meeting as "healthy Adam . . . with a voice like the thunder of God—a singer." Confirming her properly submissive domestic role, Plath writes her mother about her new appreciation of the Genesis account of woman's creation from Adam's rib: "the damn story's true!"[56] In 1956, "Ode for Ted" explicitly casts Plath's marriage within the frame of the original biblical union, and the unequal power dynamics of the pairing are uncritically presented. The authority of the speaker's Adamic mate is celebrated as he masters the land with his "least look" and summons "all earth" with "his words." The speaker's only role is to be "glad" at the prospect of Adam's exercise of power, and her only authority derives from her "lauding" of "such man's blood" (29–30). The speaker, "this adam's woman," does not even directly claim Eve's name and defines herself only in relation to her mate. Like John Milton's Eve, she seems to live and sing only for "god in him."

This conventional, sexist interpretation of the Genesis narrative of the Garden of Eden is replaced from 1956 to 1962 by less conventional meditations on marriage, and finally the biblical story of Eve's birth from Adam's rib is reenvisioned as a metaphor for self-birth. Although "Zoo Keeper's Wife" in 1961 seems to repeat the Adam's rib scenario, a dark humor edges the visceral imagery of a garden transformed into a crowded and ominous menagerie. The satanic snake who tempts Eve in the Genesis narrative appears as a "boa constrictor," and the landscape of the Garden of Paradise is reconfigured as a university's "Fellows' Garden." The burden of culpability for the fall, conventionally blamed on Eve, shifts to the Adamic figure, who, in this version, introduces her to the snake. Eve's dishonesty in the Genesis account is attributed to her temptation by the serpent, but here Eve's dishonesty is marked by her own pretense—"I pretended I was the Tree of Knowledge"—and her own agency in effecting plot: "I entered your bible, I boarded your ark" (154–155). These last lines underscore the great distance between the cliché-ridden "Ode for Ted" and Plath's later revisionist use of biblical tropes.

First, by collapsing the biblical garden with the fellows' garden, Plath implies that both biblical and academic authority are male preserves that are less than Edenic for women. Second, Eve's admission of agency and pretense complicates the traditional interpretation of her as spiritually and intellectual gullible. Her revelation of her agency here disrupts the masculine power of "naming" that is so uncritically lauded in "Ode for Ted." This revisionist message is conveyed by several primary revisionist techniques. For example, Plath collapses two biblical narratives, Adam and Eve's story with that of Noah and the ark, to critique the underlying power dynamics of both. This debunking of biblical authority gains speed and sharpness with the deflation of biblical language to the colloquial tone appropriate to "the Small Mammal House." Finally, domination, Adam's dominion over the earth and his mate, which was uncritically assumed to be a basis for marriage in "Ode for Ted," is here presented as an ugly reality that makes marriage into a cage in which the zookeeper houses his wife among his other charges.

The hermeneutics of suspicion that informs "Zoo Keeper's Wife" opens up the space for a reconstruction of meaning, a retelling of Eve's creation in Plath's later work. In 1962's "Getting There," the earth is mud, "thick, red, and slipping." No longer under Adam's foot, it is instead "Adam's side" and the site of Eve's emergence: "This earth I rise from, and I in agony" (247). Here, the Genesis story of creation fuses with the gospel's relation of Christ's agony and resurrection. The reborn woman, therefore, bears both the traits of mortal Eve and the traces of the immortal aspect of Christ. In general, this evolution in Plath's use of the figure of Eve and the Garden of Eden story anticipates key issues in the two predominate and intertwined trajectories of her biblical revision. The later figures of Eve reflect Plath's development of a hermeneutics of suspicion, a growing critique of androcentrism, and suspicion about the ability of texts of the patriarchal canon to represent women's stories. The fact that she does not abandon the Eve trope, however, is topographical evidence of a subterranean hermeneutics of desire that seeks to find some way to make the ancient text signify authentically for her, to speak to her needs, and, as Plath wanted her poems to do, to "speak of her" (142). The blending of biblical figures across gender lines (Eve with Christ) and the placement of these figures in contemporary contexts and discourses, similarly, are essential aspects of the revisionist's effort to dislocate traditional significations of the ancient myth and graft them onto and craft them into different stories.

Plath's question in November of 1962—"Who are these pietàs?"—caps a year of poetic meditation on pregnancy and childbirth that often exposes and challenges the influence of interpretations of the biblical figure of the Madonna and child on the ideology of womanhood and maternity in the 1950s. Plath begins in October 1960, just six months after the birth of her daughter, with "Magi," an outright assault on the conventional narrative of the visit of the wise men to the infant Christ. Plath asserts that the purity and innocence associated with that religious tableau depends upon a renunciation, an eradication, of the embodied reality of newborns. The "star" that "these papery godfolk" "mistake" is their worship of "abstracts." The "Good" and "the True" are "Salutary and pure as boiled water, / Loveless as the multiplication table." The sterility of their belief system is explicitly linked to the Platonic tradition of ideal forms and contrasted with the enfleshed knowledge of the child, for whom "Love the mother of milk" is "no theory" (148).

The indictment of the Western philosophical tradition for its promotion of a dichotomy between mind and body and its devaluation of the body becomes an overtly gendered critique of Christian tradition in the final stanza, where the Magi seek

> some lamp-headed Plato
> Let them astound his heart with their merit.
> What girl ever flourished in such company? (148)

If the Messiah had come as a girl, Plath implies, the gatekeepers of religion would never have recognized either her genius or her divinity. Indeed, the poem bitterly indicts the shared assumptions and masculinist bias of Western philosophical and religious tradition. The "papery godfolk" Plath challenges, however, are not just the characters of the wise men in the New Testament or the texts of Platonic philosophy. This poem also engages the papery godfolk of literary tradition, specifically the wise men of modernism.

Plath's ambivalent relation to her male modernist precursors is marked here by this poem's dialogue with Eliot's sobering dramatic monologue in "The Journey of the Magi" and with Yeats's frightening evocation of a nightmarish millennium in "The Second Coming." Eliot's Magi's nostalgia for "the old dispensation" and the closing image of "an alien people clutching their gods" certainly presents the biblical narrative in an unconventional and disturbing light.[57] The realism evoked by Eliot's first-person narration and gritty description of the journey enhances the credibility of the poem's version of the event and its depiction of the historical reticence of cultures to accept change. This revision of the New Testament narratives of the wise men's journey refuses a mystical joy at the Messiah's birth and underscores the pain of changing orders. Plath borrows and intensifies these elements of Eliot's reimagination of the scene and redirects the political critique toward gender. Eliot's Magi might indeed have been "glad of another death" if they had found a female messiah in the holy crib.

Similarly, Plath's "Magi" radically reshapes Yeats's famous question: "What rough beast, its hour come round at last / Slouches towards Bethlehem to be born?" If Plath intensifies and reconfigures Eliot's critique, she deflates and mocks Yeats's nightmare. Because of the strong association of femaleness with carnality in the philosophical tradition Plath satirizes, the femaleness of the child god of her poem may cause the wise men to view the baby as a "rough beast." The subcurrent of humor in Plath's "Magi," however, derives from the speaker's delighted assertion of the beastliness, the innocent animality, of her child. The monstrous evil lurking in Yeats's "rocking cradle" is gently lampooned by this figure of a strong and healthy six-month-old:

> she is able
> To rock on all fours like a padded hammock.
> For her, the heavy notion of Evil
> Attending her cot is less than a belly ache. (148)

In "Heavy Women," which also engages both the Bible and Yeats, the pregnant women "listen for the millennium," but in a reversal of Yeats's "Second Coming," the ominous approaching figures are the "wise gray men" who are "bearing down" as the "axle of winter / Grinds round" (158). Thus, Plath's revision of the work of her modernist precursors is part and parcel of her biblical revision in "Magi" and "Heavy Women," just as the biblical critique is related to and fostered by a critique of some of the cornerstones of Western philosophy.

The sous-ratour structure of revision here appears in the simultaneous evocation and revocation of traditional readings of the New Testament. The ambivalence that allows this narrative strategy is also evidenced by more conventional uses of this ancient script elsewhere in Plath's work. A year after "Magi," Plath evokes the manger scene as lovingly as a lullaby, as conventionally as a nursery rhyme. In "Nick and the Candlestick" (240–242), the "blood blooms clean" in the male infant who offers the Christ child's traditional promise of hope for the future. He is "the one / Solid the spaces lean on, envious." His is "the baby in the barn." While this closing image offers a standard depiction of the divine baby, this poem does not signal a retreat from biblical revision. Instead, it points to another current in the stream of Plath's reimagination of the significance of the Madonna and child. If the infant is Christ, the speaker is Mary. The purity that was shown to be so problematic in "Magi" similarly ignites a revision of the figure of the Virgin Mother and her relation to the sexualized split between virgins and whores in Western culture.

"Heavy Women" (158) opens with the traditional image of pregnant women as pensive and peaceful, "smiling to themselves," meditating "Devoutly as the Dutch bulb / Forming its twenty petals," only to debunk that iconographic tradition. The poem suggests that actual heavy women are misrepresented by the figure of the Madonna. "Mary-blue" is a "dusk" that "hoods" and thereby obscures the actual women as they "step among the archetypes." The superfluity of cherubim, the artistic flourishes gracing traditional representation of the Virgin, underscores the inanity of this representation: "Pink-buttocked infants attend them . . . doing nothing in particular." The virginal purity satirized here is fiercely indicted over a year later in "Fever 103" (231–232). That poem's opening interrogation of the meaning of purity culminates in the emergence of "a pure acetylene / Virgin." Though this virgin is still attended by useless "cherubim," or "whatever these pink things mean," she clearly disdains them, and as she denies a masculine trinity of "him"s, they "dissolve" with her "old whore" selves. Although this acetylene virgin still is defined in opposition to the whore, the speaker implies that part of her former corruption was the fetishized purity of the traditional representation of the Madonna.

The switch from third to first person marks the progression in the fury of the critique of the Madonna archetype from "Heavy Women" to "Fever 103." With the reserve and self-consciousness prized by the New Critics, the speaker looks at the archetype of "Heavy Women." Thus, that poem itself can only gingerly "step through" the gallery of those archetypes. That distance evaporates, however, in the later poems as the archetypes themselves speak and transform the icon to iconoclast. This movement can be traced through the progression of the speaking subject and the subject of her speech, motherhood as patriarchal institution heavily influenced by the biblical figure of the Madonna and child, from "Three Women" to "Medusa" and finally to the pair of innocence and experience in "Morning Song" and "Mary's Song."

The voices of "Three Women: A Poem for Three Voices" (176–187) present a triptych of revisionist perspectives on the tradition of Madonna and child that balances a critique of the social construction of maternity with an awe for this primary female power. Axelrod describes this poem as a departure for Plath in its placing of "women at the center of the symbolic order, substituting a trinity of female originators for the male myth of origins."[58] The imagery evoked by the first voice, that of a laboring woman, hints at the mythic precursors of the Virgin Mary in Greek and Near Eastern goddess traditions. The second voice, that of a woman suffering miscarriage, metaphorizes patriarchal control of reproduction in terms of masculine divine patrilineage. The third voice, that of a woman who gives up her newborn, critiques the Annunciation and returns to the meditation on women and knowledge begun in "Zoo Keeper's Wife" and "Heavy Women." Stylistically, the intercutting of these monologues achieves a double effect. While it makes the different colors of their critiques refract one another like stained glass in a mosaic or a church window, it also underscores the speakers' isolation from one another and the fragmentary nature of their individual understandings.[59]

Whereas the first voice approaches her labor with the "calm" of the virginal archetypes of "Heavy Women" (she too is hooded in "blue" like "a Mary"), her composure is merely the calm before "something awful." Her isolation in the delivery room—she is "set apart"—further marks her resemblance to Mary, who is set apart from other women. The speaker's sense of herself as "sacrificial," however, points not only to Mary's service in the divine plan, but to Christ's. This is a key aspect of Plath's revision: she blends the Madonna not only with the whore in some poems, but also with the divine child, thereby deifying the mother figure. The later usurpation of Christ's identity is hinted at here as the laboring woman sacrifices her body, like Christ, bearing "a cargo of agony" through this "cruel" "miracle." As the woman's body is split in childbirth, the imagery used to present her splits the Mary figure into the goddess traditions that it absorbed and repressed. Like Demeter, she is the nurturing mother earth, declaring herself a "sky and hill of good," "a wall and roof, protecting." Like the myth of the formation of land and sky from the breaking apart of the Near Eastern goddess Tiamat's body, the speaker announces, "I am breaking apart like the world." And echoing Eve's curse, the knowledge that her progeny must be brought forth in suffering to suffer, she asks, "What pains, what sorrows must I be mothering?" This evocation and blending of goddesses and biblical foremothers is disrupted by the figure of the mother as victim of maternity. The speaker realizes "I am the center of an atrocity" and, horrified, asks, "Can such innocence kill and kill?" Here, the infant appears like the terrorizing, dictatorial Christ child of Sexton's "Jesus Suckles," who proclaims: "I am a truck. I run everything. / I own you" (338). This eruption of protest is recontained postpartum as Plath's speaker pushes her realization into "dreams" of "terrible children" while she decorates her nursery with the "little hearts," the cultural iconography of happy 1950s motherhood.

The patriarchal context for motherhood is made blatantly evident by the second voice, who connects her infertility to that of one-dimensional, male professional types, businessmen and doctors, who are "jealous gods / That would have the whole world flat because they are." The male gods' pure disembodiedness recalls the sterility of the Magi's preference for a "lamp-headed Plato."

> I see the Father conversing with the Son.
> Such flatness cannot but be holy.
> "Let us make a heaven," they say.
> "Let us flatten and launder the grossness from these souls."
> (179)

Reading this voice in concert with "Magi" reveals a sustained critique of the flesh loathing of Western religious tradition and an assertion that the religious iconography of mother and child is really about patrilineage, the original creation of the Son by the Father alone.

This critique brings forth a countertype, a female figure defined in opposition to the sterile, clean, and genteel Father and Son. This figure combines the earth mother tradition, evoked also by the first voice, with that of the carnal, rapacious woman who appears in midrash as Lilith, in Milton as Sin, and as the

Tooth-Mother, or mother of death, in contemporary poetry by writers like Robert Bly. Plath's figure marks the bridge between the critique of Virgin and child iconography and her (re)construction of a female deity. While she appears negatively as the "dark earth" and "the vampire of us all," she has also been victimized by what Enid Dame's "Lilith" calls "bad press."[60] Having been used "meanly" by men, the threat of her revenge is underscored with chantlike repetition: "She will eat them. / Eat them, eat them, eat them in the end." This little mother of death will be resurrected in the creative burst of October 1962, as the ascending figure of "Lady Lazarus" echoes her vow to "eat men like air."

If the purity and flatness of the traditional representation of the masculine Trinity requires the representation of its female opposite, the grossly enfleshed mother of death, it also produces another counter. The "Good" and "True" depicted in "Magi" as the foundation of divine masculine patrilineage is indicted by the third voice of "Three Women" on the charge of rape. Just as "Magi" entered into conversation with Yeats's "The Second Coming," so this woman's narration simultaneously engages "Leda and the Swan" and the Gospels' depiction of the Annunciation. "Doves and words," as in the Gospels, bring "conceptions," but they signify only "dangers" to the speaker. This speaker's pregnancy is in fact unintended and unwanted. The angel of the Gospels, frequently depicted with wings in religious art, fuses with Yeats's divine swan in Plath's revision. The speaker remembers "a white, cold wing" and "the great swan with its terrible look, / coming at me." The "black meaning" in his "eye" mirrors Anne Sexton's revision of the Annunciation, which describes the angel's penetration of Mary with his "executioner's eyes." Sexton's implication that his fertilization is also an execution echoes Plath's speaker's claim that the fetus "murders" her. The poetic balance of the line asserting "I should have murdered this, that murders me" ironically reverses the balance and nurturance implicit in traditional representations of the babe suckling at the mother's breast.

Plath's revision in "Three Women" of that figure continues the meditation on the relationship of women to knowledge that she began in "Zoo Keeper's Wife." Just as that poem collapsed the biblical accounts of Noah and the ark with the Garden of Eden, so the divine bird of Plath's annunciation recalls the insidious tempter of Genesis: "There is a snake in swans." This line not only paints the divine messenger in a satanic light, it also connects the Genesis account of Eve's eating of the fruit of knowledge to the question Yeats raises in his version of the Greek myth as to whether the virgin "put on his knowledge with his power." Plath's emphasis on the shared assumptions of biblical myth and male modernist mythology underscores the very problem that Adrienne Rich derives from Yeats's question about women and knowledge: Do intellectual women become like the canon they consume?[61] The final appearance of the third speaker suggests that knowledge, as represented by the patriarchal academy, places women in problematic relation to their bodily creativity. After surrendering her unwanted newborn, the third voice returns to college and graduates, but this spring ritual signals not renewal, but debauchery and loss. The "colleges are drunk with spring," and the black graduation gown is "a little funeral" that shows the speaker is "serious." This woman's sacrifice of her offspring, a tangible representative of her creative power, however, coexists with repeated critiques of the self-sacrifice implicit in traditional representations of Madonna and child and the domestic ideology of angelic motherhood.

"Medusa" (224–226), originally titled "Mum: Medusa," blends Greek and Christian mythology like "Three Women"[62] but makes more explicit the Christ/Mary analogy that underlies the suffering of one of the laboring voices of "Three Women" and adds a critique of self-sacrificing piety. The speaker's interrogation of the mother's identity—"Who do you think you are?"—establishes the speaker's self-definition as one who rejects the Christlike self-sacrifice of the mother. A draft of this section even declares, "I am not pietà / I refuse to be."[63]

Similarly, the blend of biblical and Greek references here reflects the speaker's quest for an adult authority; she has "put aside childish things" along with the eerily infantile voice of "Daddy" to appropriate the literate, authoritative voice associated with Greek mythology.[64] Like the "black gown" worn by the graduating speaker of "Three Women," the classical Greek and sacred biblical myth donned (and rent) by the speaker of "Medusa" signifies to the "god-eyed ones," the literary giants Plath admired, that she is "serious."

The refusal of the speaker in this poem to partake of the "Communion wafer" of the body of "Blubbery Mary" is the speaker's attempt to reconstitute her own self. This collapse of Christ and Mary indicts the self-sacrificial Christian rhetoric supporting the construction of socially sanctioned feminine identity from the Victorian "angel in the house" to twentieth-century martyred moms. Drafts reveal Plath's decision to cross out an explicit naming of the Virgin: "I am sick to death of {maternity, you, Mary, Mary!}."[65] This blow struck against tradition, however, depends upon an equal and opposite motion, obeying the ironic logic of sous-ratour. The speaker must evoke the tradition to revoke it, and the manner in which she revokes it remakes the tradition. While the speaker rejects Mary as a "Ghastly Vatican," she nonetheless presents Mary and Christ as sharing an identity. Christ's wounds become maternal wombs as the image of the "red stigmata at the very center" is replaced by that of the "fat and red" "placenta" that miraculously walks across the ocean's water to smother the speaker.

Although "Medusa" despises the identification it recognizes between the martyred mother figure and Christ, this rejection inevitably bolsters the signifying force of this problematic blend of motherhood with Christian sacrifice. Plath's rejection of the mother, however, only ensures her "perpetual presence," just as it inadvertently ensures the continuation of the masochistic figure of the Christlike woman. Despite her attempts to cast off this figure, Plath's Medusa, her "Ghastly Vatican," remains, as Sexton phrases it, "my Lady of my first words" (46). The ascending female deities that close many of the poems Plath composed in 1962, shortly after "Medusa," similarly appropriate attributes of Christ, although they increasingly foreground divinity and wisdom as well as suffering. This marks the shift in Plath's revision, most notable in the poems of October 1962, from the figure of Madonna and child to that of a female deity. "Mary's Song," written in November, offers a brief return to the mother-child line, but with the important addition of Holocaust tropes. This final example of Plath's revision of Madonna and child will demonstrate how the Holocaust tropes function as catalyst, completing the transformation of the Madonna from saint to goddess.

Although readers may not immediately connect the mild, if unconventional, depiction of motherhood of "Morning Song" (156–157) with the apocalyptic scene of "Mary's Song" (257), the two poems may be seen as companion pieces, like Blake's "Songs of Innocence" and "Songs of Experience." Plath chose "Morning Song" to open her arrangement of *Ariel* with the word "love," and it offers a careful portrait of the integrity and individuality of infants even as it broaches its subject in ways that were unconventional for its time.[66] "Mary's Song," written over a year later, more obviously recalls Blake's "Songs of Experience" in its use of Christian imagery to show the world's slaughter of innocents. Despite the poem's different tones, several common elements suggest that they can profitably be read in tandem.

The first line of "Morning Song"—"Love set you going like a fat gold watch"—suggests an absent clock-maker God as well as the human lovemaking that initiates life. But this life source may be only a kinder version of the absence of goodness that allows the atrocities chronicled in "Mary's Song." The fact of the infant's separateness in "Morning Song," that his cry must take its "place among the elements," anticipates his inevitable journey beyond parental care. The absence of a personal deity and the inevitable separation of parent and child in the earlier poem are necessary precursors to the world of the later poem, just as innocence is a necessary precursor to experience. The images of "Mary's Song" also expressly echo "Morning Song." The image of the "fat gold watch" breaks down in the later poem as the symbolic "lamb" cooks in "fat" and "The fat / Sacrifices its opacity" and seems to become "A window, holy gold." Furthermore, the distance between the tones of the two poems is not that great. The earlier poem, after all, is no joyous aubade. While the voice we hear is that of the mother, "cowheavy," as she goes to nurse her infant, the morning song to which the title refers is the child's dawn cries as he tries his "handful of notes." While the image of the child's "vowels" rising "like balloons" is ostensibly a hopeful ending as his song grows with the daylight, the daybreak itself is described in disturbing images: the "window square / Whitens and swallows its dull stars." This ambivalence thus provides an undertone of mourning or dread in this "Morning Song."

If the realism of "Morning Song" deflates the 1950s glorified representations of motherhood, the surrealism of "Mary's Song" deromanticizes traditional representations of Madonna and child. The force and impact of the later poem derive from its casting of domestic and maternal tragedy within figures from the Holocaust. Written just five days after "Death and Company" (which explicitly refers to Blake), the "Sunday lamb" cracking "in its fat" opens the poem with an ironic reference to the innocence of Blake's "little lambs."

Although critics have chastised Plath for casting personal sorrows in the Holocaust tropes, the poem's strength derives from its apocalyptic vision. As the concentration camp "ovens glowed like heavens," the speaker declares: "It is a heart, / This holocaust I walk in." Plath's imagery shares with Blake's "A Divine Image" a stark horror and visionary indictment of human atrocity. Rather than a reflection of God, Blake casts the "Human Heart" as the "hungry Gorge," or passageway to the "seal'd" "Furnace" that is the "Human Face." Plath's holocaust "heart" similarly indicts the falseness of humanity as it recognizes the pervasiveness of evil and the failure of humanity to recognize divinity; the "world" will "kill and eat" the "golden child." While references to the divine child open and close the poem, unlike the "baby in the barn" that closes "Nick and the Candlestick," he promises no salvation or hope. Even as the last line evokes him ("O golden child"), it predicts his death, his uselessness. He can well be dispensed with because this poem is not, finally, about him, but about Mary. It is, after all, her song. The assertion of the enormity of her suffering fore-grounds her as a tragic figure, not only larger than the victims of the Holocaust, but also larger than Christ, even as these tropes wrench the spotlight away from the historical victims of Nazi atrocities and the "golden child."[67]

This representational strategy that both evokes and elides the traditional deity anticipates the fate of the ascending female deity that dominates the conclusions of the poems written in that furious burst of creativity in October 1962. As Pamela Annas notes, a "protean female protagonist, hero, victim, god-dess" takes center stage.[68] At this time, the "Girl who wanted to be God" finally felt sure of her "genius," even predicting to her mother that these poems would "make [her] name."[69] The sense of authority demonstrated by this quotation also charac-terizes the way the poetry of the period increasingly links po-etic authority with the body, particularly an ascending female body. Susan Van Dyne asserts that in these poems, "bodily au-thority came to stand for poetic authority" as Plath reimagined traditional constructions of the female, sexual body.[70] In this fusion of poetic, material, and spiritual subjectivity, we can see Plath's contribution to the growing insistence among twenti-eth-century women poets that "God and the imagination and *my body* are one."[71]

The imaginative challenge of this project, however, derives from the fact that the building materials available overwhelm-ingly come from dominant cultural and literary tradition, which denigrates women's flesh. Lant, in fact, persuasively demonstrates that the trope of "nakedness" for self-revelation that was so widely used by Plath's male contemporaries could not be used in the same way by her to reveal a female self.[72] The disempowering tradition of representations of female disembodiedness in patriarchal culture and literature render the signification of that flesh problematic. The "I" that so much wanted to write its own character and role in Plath's teenage journal entry does indeed find its "power" already "quantified" and "qualified" as the speaking subject struggles to redefine itself in the late work. Ironically, Plath's very turn to the body as a vehicle for representing her transformed and transforming subject eventually requires the erasure of the materiality of that subject. Despite her critique, evidenced by poems like "Magi," of the traditional valuation of disembodiedness by Western philosophical and religious tradition, her attempts to ground authority in the material "I" repeatedly end with the transformation of powerful body into pure spirit, into nothing. Thus, the self-canceling structure of sous-ratour is in place as Lady Lazarus rises, the arrow flies into the sun, the murderess finds her heaven, and the lioness "melts to a shriek."

Plath's revisionist poems that witness the emergence of a female deity ultimately also bear the inscription of the narratives of Western philosophy that demand the erasure of the flesh and the nineteenth-century novels that frequently end with the heroine's death. However, these poems' revisionist energy enables them to break the "sentence" of traditional representations of women and challenge the "sequence," although, due to their sous-ratour structure, they ironically reiterate the effect of that sequence.[73]

Intimations of the new subject who emerges in October of 1962 appear even in Plath's juvenilia; remember the "outrageous nimble queen" of "Aerialist." While the "descending angel" of "Black Rook" in 1956 evidences an openness to revelation, it is not until 1960 that an ascending angel appears. Again, maternity seems to have been the issue that triggers the speaker's deific self-description. At the conclusion of "Love

Letter"—likely an address to a child who has figuratively awak-
ened her—the speaker describes her ascension in terms that
foreshadow the late work:

> From stone to cloud, so I ascended.
> Now I resemble a sort of god
> Floating through the air in my soul-shift
> Pure as a pane of ice. It's a gift. (147)

The icy purity of this "sort of god" anticipates the "acetylene
Virgin" who ascends at the end of "Fever 103." The pun on
"soul-shift"—a mystical transformation represented in the garb
of a lady's housedress or "shift"—and the light self-deprecation
of the closing couplet hint at the mocking vernacular that
reaches its sharpest edge in Lady Lazarus's performance "for
the peanut-crunching crowd."

Three of the "Bee poems"—"The Bee Meeting," "The Arrival of the Bee Box," and "Stings" (211–215)—written early in
October, set the pattern for revisions of that month. The "virgin" bees dream of a duel with the queen and the resulting
"bride flight": the "upflight of the murderess into a heaven that
loves her." This description interestingly offers a glimpse into
the process of revision itself since it suggests the hermeneutics
of both suspicion and desire. The "murder" of the power of the
traditional order qualifies as an act of rebellion that depends
upon the ground of suspicion and critique of that order. The
outcome of reward, rather than penalty, for this rebellion evidences the workings of the hermeneutics of desire. As Van
Dyne argues, the "Queen's 'more terrible' need is to reinscribe
her identity on the heavens."[74] Here is constructed a "heaven"
that will welcome the murderess, the iconoclast.

It may be appropriate that Plath's speaker presents herself as
"murderess," since she may be acting out the wish of one of the
speakers of "Three Women" to "murder this, that murders
me." As noted in chapter 1, the surface text of the Bible may
bear the traces of a long-repressed murder, the appropriation

and masking of Near Eastern and Greek female deities. The ascending woman speaker of the October poems may, like the narrator of one of Plath's short stories, be "recreating dreams" that are no longer "written down" but still "shadow themselves forth in the vaguest way."[75] These shadows of goddess figures in the iconography even of the Virgin Mary may be the divine spark radiating from the ascending figures, beginning with the queen bee. This "bride flight" indeed provides the poem's emotional climax. This momentary triumphant ascension of the bee is only imagined by the speaker here, who ends, exhausted and cold, wondering about the function of a suspiciously coffinlike box.

"The Arrival of the Bee Box" witnesses a growth in the speaker's power, as she decides the "box" is "only temporary," and she will be able to "be sweet God," freeing the bees. Finally in "Stings," the speaker crosses the bridge from observation to identification and action. Like the progression in the first trajectory of revision of the Madonna and child from third-person to first-person narration and the consequent escalation in critique, so the ascending female deity here gains her own voice.

In "Stings," she first watches the tattered queen, "her wings torn shawls." Then, the speaking subject becomes the subject of her speech:

> I am no drudge
> Though for years I have eaten dust
> And dried plates with my dense hair. (214)

This image brilliantly conflates the gospel's depiction of Mary Magdalene's service to Christ with the drudgery of a modern Cinderella trapped in the kitchen. Although this stanza distinguishes the "I" who is "in control" of the "honey-machine" from the "honey-drudgers," she too has been a servant, a drudge, but now seeks to revive her regal identity:

I

Have a self to recover, a queen

. . . .

Where has she been,
With her lion-red body, her wings of glass?

Now she is flying
More terrible than she ever was, red
Scar in the sky, red comet
Over the engine that killed her—
The mausoleum, the wax house. (215)

This closing image, the flight frozen in time, inaugurates the pattern repeated in "Fever 103," "Ariel," and "Lady Lazarus." This freeze-frame technique provides the sense of agency even as it records the disappearance of the speaker. She is flying "now" even though we learn that she already has been "killed." Similarly, Ariel's flight into the sun asserts her brilliance even as it necessitates her death. In summary, these poems repeatedly end with the "ending" of the speaker even though the power of the ascending figure offers a sense of agency and even kinetic energy.[76]

Furthermore, the "flight" that closes "Stings" anticipates the imagery of the other October poems. The "lion-red" body of "Stings" figures again as God's lioness in "Ariel" and as veiled lioness of "Purdah," while the color red ("red scar," "red comet") later describes Lady Lazarus's fearsome mane. Finally, the assertion that this ascending figure is "More terrible than she ever was" reveals the most basic, underlying similarity among the revisionist October poems. As Gilbert argues, the "mausoleum," over which the figure flies, may be the house of literary history, another "wax house." Just a month after writing these poems, Plath literalized that relation, renting a flat that once had been part of Yeats's actual abode.[77] I would contend that the intertextual figure who emerges and ascends in the October poetry responds to the "terrible beauty" born in

Yeats's "Easter 1916," just as "Magi" responds to "The Second Coming." As we saw with "Magi," Plath's biblical revision depends upon a fusion and reshaping of figures from other traditions, such as Near Eastern and Greek goddess traditions, as well as the literary mythology in her own backyard, the male modernists. The figure distilled from these component traditions and charged with the apocalyptic heat of Holocaust tropes need not ask, as Lady Lazarus does, "Do I terrify?" Van Dyne asserts that the word "terrible" signified for Plath both "rebellion" and the awareness that such rebellious desire was "monstrous."[78] Yeats's "terrible beauty" of tragic, political self-sacrifice born in "Easter of 1916" thus becomes in Plath's October poems a resurrected female deity who similarly unleashes awesome furor and power even as she chronicles her disappearance.

"Fever 103" (231–232), written on October 20, 1962, picks up where the Madonna and child line of revision leaves off. While this poem's meditation on purity and corruption makes use of the traditional opposition between virgins and whores, it problematizes that juxtaposition of the two and the traditional significance of the Virgin. The movement of the poem from the opening questioning of the meaning of purity to the closing ascension of an "acetylene Virgin" is sped by the use of tropes on the destruction inflicted by the dropping of the atomic bomb in World War II. Adulterers' bodies are "greased" with radiation like "Hiroshima ash," and their "sin" is "eating in," melting or consuming their flesh. Here is another holocaust for the speaker's heart to "walk in." Then the poem makes the significant step we noticed in Plath's earlier Madonna revision, from third to first person. The speaker's "I" takes center stage, and it is as if the radiation that evidenced the defilement of the adulterers has become a radiant light signifying her purity. As in "Medusa" and "Three Women," the speaker also assumes aspects of Christ, but the figuration here is much bolder. The speaker's "Three days. Three nights" of suffering suggest the three-day period between Christ's crucifixion and resurrection. The passage of this time also marks the emergence of the proof of her divinity. Like "God," she is injured by the "world," by the flesh; and like the Gospels' promise of Christ as a light unto the world's paths, so she is a "lantern" exuding incredible light. Again, the radiation that signified corruption in earlier stanzas seems to be appropriated and transformed by the speaker into her own astounding "heat" and "light." The transformation of radiation into radiance evidences the function of Holocaust tropes here as a catalyst on biblical revision. It is this radiance that propels her ascension, her "rise," as the "beads of hot metal fly."

This ascension marks the difference between this poem and the earlier revisionist trajectory of the Madonna and child. While this poem shares the critiques of pietàs, as the "cherubim" attending her are ridiculed as meaningless "pink things," it goes further in the apprehension of Mary. Mary's ascension, traditionally part of Catholic doctrine, replaces Christ's here as her "selves" dissolve "To Paradise." Van Dyne perceptively remarks that the stereotypical virgin associated with "absence or unconscious materiality" is "recast" here into a "wounding presence and the agent of its own ecstatic excess."[79] The trinity of "him"s the speaker denies—"Not you, nor him / Not him, nor him"—refers back in the poem to the adulterers and seals a delayed rhyme with the "The sin. The sin." But it also refuses a masculine trinity, linking them to her old "selves," "old whore petticoats," significantly shifting the burden of corruption, of whorishness, onto the male. The reiterated denial of the masculine figure anticipates the peeling away of "dead stringencies" in "Ariel" that similarly releases that speaker's flight.

The ascending figure of "Ariel" is the most positive and palatable of this line, but she is just the shiny side of the vengeful Lady Lazarus. As Kroll demonstrates, Plath adopts all the diverse aspects of the moon goddess.[80] The title "Ariel" evokes the terrible aspect of the white goddess because it refers not only to Shakespeare's *Tempest* but to "fiery sacrifice, purification, and transcendence" associated with her name in the

Bible.[81] Furthermore, as the "arrow that flies" into "morning," the speaker also appropriates a phallic image from Plath's *The Bell Jar*. This speaker fulfills Esther Greenwood's wish to be the arrow, not the place from which it shoots.[82] But she also fills the space left by an absent deity in the earlier poem "Widow," where the "draftiness" of "God's voice" allows "no bodies, singing like arrows up to heaven" (164). The flight of this arrow, bound like that of "Bee Meeting" for a "heaven that loves her," is also "Suicidal" in its "drive" into the sun. Therefore, like the dissolving "I" of "Fever 103," the iteration of "I" in "Ariel" marks both the speaker's divine transformation and her erasure. The "I" that sheds "dead stringencies," becomes "Foam to wheat" and finally is the "arrow" that merges with the "red Eye," the sun. While this merger signals the speaker's destruction, it also suggests an immortal "eye," a fixed image of this flight. The self-canceling sous-ratour structure here is apparent.

"Purdah" (242–244), written just two days later, continues the play on identity and vision, troping on the Hindu tradition of covering women's faces. The speaker declares: "My eye / Veil is." This poem, in a sense, lifts the veil of "Ariel," revealing the underside of God's pure powerful lioness to be "The lioness, / The shriek in the bath, / The cloak of holes." Perloff recognizes that the central "transformation" here draws upon the Egyptian lioness-goddess tradition and witnesses "a prelapsarian Eve" become the terrible "Clytemnestra."[83] This figure, born of the "agonized side" of "Adam," however, barely emerges and indicts the tradition of male ownership and masking of women before vanishing. The final figure, after all, is a fabric of "holes" or absences. The startling violence of her self-revelation, however, parallels the force of the self-presentation of "Lady Lazarus" (244–247), written the same week.

As the most obvious example of Plath's use of the Bible as intertext, the appropriation of the story of Lazarus's resurrection in "Lady Lazarus" offers an unmistakable performance of the revisionist's hermeneutics of suspicion. The refusal of a male trinity in "Fever 103" is more forcefully cast here as an indictment of male authority that allies medical, professional, and religious figures with male Nazis: "Herr God, Herr Lucifer." Casting Lazarus as female rather than male, her death as self-inflicted rather than natural, and Jesus as satanic death-camp physician rather than divine healer enables the final appearance of an enraged woman who seems to seek revenge for the despisal of female flesh in both the Gospels and contemporary culture.

> Out of the ash
> I rise with my red hair
> And I eat men like air. (247)

Just as "Mary's Song" draws on the horrors of the Holocaust to rewrite the pietà and offer a powerful figure of the Virgin, so "Lady Lazarus" draws on the same tropes to resurrect the figure of the whore in this closing image, evoking the Magdalene with her magnificent red hair.[84] The revisioned voice of Lazarus and the Magdalene, however, depends on yet another biblical subtext. The transformation of Lazarus's gender, through the hermeneutics of suspicion, is shaped by a cross-gender identification of the female speaker, through the hermeneutics of desire, with the sufferings of Job.[85]

Despite the seeming incongruity of Lady Lazarus's sideshow theatrics and Job's somber complaint in verses 16–17 of that biblical book,[86] the "stripped" condition of her body and soul uncannily mirrors the forced divestment of Job of all his earthly possessions. The speakers' very breath seems to be drawn from the same source. While Job declares: "My breath is corrupt, my days are extinct, / the graves are ready for me" (17.1), Lady Lazarus predicts her "sour breath / Will vanish in a day" because:

> Soon, soon the flesh
> The grave cave ate will be
> At home on me. (244)

Even Plath's figuration of grave as domestic site, as "home," offers a compressed echo of Job's ironic location of death's decay within a trope on family: "I have said to corruption, Thou art my father: and to the worm Thou art my mother" (17.13–14).

Structural similarities also point to the Book of Job as a re-visioned subtext of "Lady Lazarus." Although Job's losses are not self-inflicted, he is diminished to the point of death twice by losses of family, property, and health, and each time he, like Lady Lazarus, makes an amazing "comeback in broad day." It seems that Job too has a "call" for doing it "so that it feels like hell." Furthermore, by casting God and Lucifer as ruthless Nazis in her poem, Plath only foregrounds the collusion of God with Satan that underwrites the plot of Job. The frame narrative of the biblical text clearly states that Job's trials result from a bet between God and Satan (Job 1–2). Finally, the roots of Plath's construction of audience in "Lady Lazarus" may lie in Job's hostile relation to those who witness his spectacle.

Lady Lazarus's despisal of the "peanut-crunching crowd" that "shoves in" to gawk at her echoes Job's bitterness toward the "mockers" who surround him and "gape with open mouths" at his condition (17.2; 16.10). Yet Job, like Lady Lazarus, needs his sorrow to be self-revelation, to be public spectacle, praying that the earth never "cover" his "blood" and that his body be a "byword of the people," stirring the "inno-cent . . . against the hypocrite" (16.10; 17.6–8). This function of Job's body as a public sign of injustice merges in Plath's poem with the function of Lazarus's body as a public sign of Jesus' divinity. The Lady Lazarus who manages her own resurrection in the final moments of the poem thus appears as an avenging goddess, at once a sign of divine injustice and of feminine, supernatural power.

However, the speaker's threat to "eat men like air" is overshadowed by her self-portrayal as victim throughout the poem. The undercutting of this assertion of power may also be linked to audience, particularly to Plath's reformulation of audience in Job. The drafts of "Lady Lazarus" reveal that Plath's "fixation on a male audience for her strenuous self-proclamation" first shaped the speaker's voice against a negative audience that survives in the final draft as "Herr God, Herr Lucifer."[87] This hostile audience seems in the drafts of "Lady Lazarus" to perform the function of the "mockers" exemplified in Job by his wife, who sneers: "Dos't thou still retain thine integrity? Curse God and Die" (2.9). I propose that Plath recontains the integrity of her speaker's voice by collapsing the split in Job between dramatic speaker and mocking audience into her own parodic dramatic monologue. However, by internalizing the mocking voice of the hostile audience in her own parodic performance, it may be that Lady Lazarus paradoxically follows the advice of Job's wife to curse God and die. This cancellation of the voice is further complicated by other strains in Plath's heteroglossia, particularly her use of images from the Holocaust.

Clearly, the Holocaust tropes are used to present the figure of female rage over gender atrocity. Every reader leaves this poem with the sense of witnessing a battle, and the closing threat of eating "men like air" seems to target a male enemy. However, despite Lady Lazarus's militant feminist anger, a closer examination of the poem reveals that the wrongs that motivate the speaker are never directly named.

Especially striking is the absence of an explicit articulation of gender critique. The universal sense that this is a poem of sexual battle, in fact, is incongruous with the actual rhetoric of the poem. This representational paradox stems from a confusion of subjects as the figure of the Holocaust victim is used to present the figure of a wronged woman. While the title presents a female speaker, Lady Lazarus's own descriptions present herself as "a smiling woman," "the same, identical woman," or as a Jewish Holocaust victim: with "skin / Bright as a Nazi lampshade," a "face," like a "fine / Jew linen," and a self like a "pure gold baby." In other words, I suggest that the speaker's gender identity is not consonant with her Jewish identity. This is not to say that the Jewish figures here are inherently male or female because, in actuality, they are overtly neither: gender is simply not foregrounded in those tropes. The "ash," the "cake of soap," the "wedding ring" evoke the "Flesh, bone" of the human victims of Nazi atrocity, but this flesh bears no expressly gendered marker. This fact points to an entanglement of tropes of ethnicity and the subject of gender. Plath may have adopted this representational strategy due to difficulties in claiming and articulating anger directly. As critics have shown, she struggled with her rage over gender inequities and saw anger, as Virginia Woolf did, as a "problem" for a woman writer who would be great.[88]

The representation of gender violence and oppression through Nazi violence, however, is the poem's genius and contributes to its powerful effect. As we saw in "Fever 103," Holocaust tropes act as a catalyst, releasing a critique of traditional biblical interpretation. Indeed, the entanglement of the subject of gender in Holocaust tropes further underscores the historical role of Christian rhetoric in both misogyny and anti-Semitism. However, this poem also bears out Young's claim that Holocaust tropes negatively shape the poet's subject.[89] Thus, Lady Lazarus's identification as a Holocaust victim colludes with the self-erasing strain of heroic martyrdom in the adoption of Christlike characteristics. Lady Lazarus's performance is achieved only through a rhetorical strategy that elides the object it presents. Plath's adoption of the Christian paradigm of life through death requires the consumption of the figure of a female deity—ironically, the very same "sacrifice" of "beautiful women" that the voice of Sexton's God requires at the end of "The Jesus Papers."

When I shared some of these ideas at a conference on literature and religion, some of my audience were surprised and a little perplexed at this grim conclusion. It is only human to want a happy ending: in this case, a celebration of the transcendent power of women's poetry. It is very important, however, for feminist criticism to face the roadblocks in the expression of women's imagination. If there is a happy ending in the biblical revision of Anne Sexton and Sylvia Plath, it lies in the rhetorical nature of their confessions—their potential impact on their hearers. Middlebrook describes Sexton's poetic bedrock as her "certainty that for every work of the human tongue, there [is] an auditor."[90] For Sexton and Plath, as for Dickinson and H.D., there was an intimate auditor who spurred their dialogues with the Bible and contemporary culture.

"Dear Max, . . . It's Our World": The Role of Sexton's and Plath's Intimate Audiences

In Maxine Kumin's copy of *The Book of Folly*, the volume in which "The Jesus Papers" first appeared, Anne Sexton wrote, "Dear Max, from now on it's our world."[91] The entitlement and achievement implied in that inscription really did belong to both poets. Though Sexton and Plath were friends during Lowell's workshop and continued to be inspired by each other's work, they were not primary readers for each other. As "intimate friends and professional allies," Kumin and Sexton, however, had been each other's most valuable source of poetic criticism and support throughout Sexton's whole career.[92] Traditionally educated and a published poet, Kumin provided crucial affirmation to Sexton's developing sense of herself as a writer. "Dear Max" was the key enabling auditor for her friend's audacious biblical critiques and desperate prayers, just as Sue Gilbert enabled Dickinson's work and Bryher aided H.D.'s.

Kumin helped Sexton see poetry as a "vocation," just as Dr. Orne, her psychologist, had first helped her to see poetry as therapy.[93] Eventually, the importance of audience to her authority bothered Sexton; she complained to her therapist that her "whole career as a writer" came from the "big cheat" of transference because she had "made up a poet, Anne Sexton, who would be worth something" to her doctor.[94] Clearly, Sexton longed for an essential writerly "I" that would exist independently of audience, just as she longed for an authoritarian God that could exist independently from his human creations and audience. Yet it was her need for audience that shaped her genius at performance. Confession, after all, requires a confessor. Though she ultimately was troubled by the roots of her poetic "I" in the therapist-client relationship, her relationship with Kumin offered a model for a dialogic basis of authority—the workshop—that was endorsed by the poets she revered.

Anne Sexton was just beginning her career when she met Kumin in John Holmes's poetry workshop in 1957. The pair became great friends, swapping clothes and child care, even collaborating on three children's books to make money. Their most intense and extended exchange, however, was their ongoing, informal poetry workshop throughout the sixties and early seventies. Sexton said in a 1963 interview that "whoever God is I keep making telephone calls" to him.[95] Before and after that interview, though, it is more likely that she was actually on the phone with Kumin. The two had a telephone line installed expressly for reading drafts to each other. This phone line functioned much like the mailboxes that connected Dickinson and Gilbert, but it perhaps facilitated more immediate and extended revision. Kumin recollects that they often went through "half-a-dozen revisions" of a poem. Surely this oral workshop shaped their craft; Kumin testifies to the benefits of listening rather than reading for revision of "intentional or unwanted musical devices," for example.[96] Such a sympathetic auditor, moreover, likely had a shaping effect on Sexton's daring choices of subject matter, as well as on the form of her work.

The composition of *The Awful Rowing to God* offers a striking example of Sexton's reliance on Kumin's support and judgment. In January 1973, as Sexton drafted the poems that became that volume, Kumin was writer-in-residence at a college in Kentucky. Sexton called her regularly at five o'clock "to go over the day's work."[97] Kumin not only attended the birth of this volume, but guarded its maturation from other, less sympathetic, auditors. The poet James Wright harshly criticized large sections of the manuscript. The manuscript's margins became a battleground for Kumin's and Wright's conflicting readings. The final volume includes several poems Sexton at first cut due to Wright's disapproval but readmitted after "Dear Max" argued for them.[98] The secret to the success of their long workshop, according to Kumin, was that while they critiqued each other's craft, they did not "trespass on style and voice"; in other words, they respected each other's poetic core.[99]

Because of their intimate involvement in each other's work, Kumin was the appropriate choice to write the introduction to Sexton's *Complete Poems.* Ted Hughes performs the same function for Sylvia Plath's *Collected Poems* and even edits them as well, although many feel this to be a decidedly inappropriate role for him. Hughes's control of Plath's literary estate outrages many feminist readers and scholars because of the couple's bitter separation and the conjecture that he may have contributed to her mental illness and suicide. For the years of their marriage, however, Hughes was Plath's most intimate auditor and continued to play an important role in her composition process even after their separation.

When Plath married Hughes in 1956 she dreamed of a mutually supportive union of poets who would together make a "bookshelf" of poems and a "batch" of beautiful children. After Hughes's *The Hawk in the Rain* won a *Harper's* publication contest, Plath described her elation in her journal:

All my pat theories against marrying a writer dissolve with Ted: his rejections more than double my sorrow and his acceptances rejoice me more than mine—it is as if he is the perfect male counterpart to my own self.[100]

Such rhapsodies give way quickly, though. In the very next entry, Plath admits this vision of her marriage may be only a "wish-dream" (154). The reality was that Hughes's greater success in the first few years of their marriage and the pressure of the traditionally subordinate wifely role created an unequal power dynamic. Hughes set poetic exercises for her and "disciplined" her study; Plath sometimes acted as secretary for him, typing drafts. A later, more sobering, journal entry confesses: "He is a genius. I his wife."[101]

Such a sense of inequality was inevitable given Hughes's ties to the British literary establishment. Published by Eliot's press, Hughes was a flesh and blood representation of the authority of the masculine canon. As such, he played an important role in Plath's dialogue with the Bible because, as we saw earlier, biblical authority symbolized for her the literary authority she coveted and finally appropriated. Recall her Garden of Eden poem, "Ode for Ted," written the year of their marriage, which offers her mate as the true "singer" and presents herself as only "Adam's woman." Axelrod's psychoanalytic reading of Plath's life and work asserts that in marrying Hughes, she really sought to "marry poetry."[102] Though the poetic union and marriage had failed by 1962, Hughes remained key to Plath's creative process; a Hughes-like figure appears in Plath's late work often as an audience and sometimes as a character. Ironically, as the intimate auditor became the intimate enemy, Plath found her strongest voice.

The beginnings of that voice are clearly audible in 1961's "Zoo Keeper's Wife." Recall how the speaker here distances herself from her role as "Adam's woman" in the earlier Garden of Eden poem and now identifies with Satan instead. The culmination of her trespass here is her entering of "your bible," her boarding of "your ark." The implied audience is both Noah and Hughes, who was by then strongly identified with the figures of animals in his own poems. Van Dyne's study of Plath's drafts suggests that Hughes's work functioned literally as a palimpsest that Plath wrote over. Some of Plath's most devastating appraisals of a Hughes-like figure in such poems as "Daddy" and "The Applicant" were drafted on the back of a manuscript of Hughes's own play *The Calm*.[103] More importantly, Plath's habit of writing on the back of Hughes's texts may have allowed her to literally write back to the authority he represented. The signature voice of the "Ariel poems" emerges on the reverse side of two other texts: one representing

Hughes's success in 1961 and the other representing her own with *The Bell Jar*.[104] Most significantly, the drafts of "Lady Lazarus" testify to the gradual writing out of a Hughes-like auditor whom the speaker loves masochistically. The supernatural woman of the final draft was in an earlier draft "a wax madonna" who loved her "great enemy" and the death that killed her "like a lover." Van Dyne shows how Plath's cutting out of the figure of this intimate audience/enemy allows the speaker's anger to target a larger evil: "Herr God, Herr Lucifer." Although Hughes certainly was not by this time the supportive listener that Kumin always was for Sexton, he functions as a key audience for the rage and indictment central to Plath's biblical revision.

In an important sense, both Kumin and Hughes have played a mediating role in the circulation of Sexton's and Plath's work. Despite their different circumstances, they stood in for the other audiences the poets hoped to address; and in different ways, they contributed to the poets' constructions of authority. Kumin has continued to help Sexton reach a greater audience by writing about her and working with scholars interested in her. However, Hughes, Plath's literary executor, admitted to destroying some manuscripts and has been accused of denying some scholars access to her work.[105] One can only wonder how the legacy of Plath's biblical revision would be different if she had had a different intimate audience.

The importance of these flesh and blood auditors for the biblical revision of Sexton and Plath, as well as of Dickinson and H.D., may be in part attributable to the dearth of textual traditions offering an alternative to the canonical model for authority. Their work, however, contributes to the building of just such a tradition, and evidence of their influence is readily visible in the work of many American women poets since 1970. The next chapter examines the work of two women novelists who did have access to an alternative tradition, and we will weigh the significance of that textual audience on their biblical revision.

Notes

1. Anne Sexton, *The Complete Poems*, ed. Linda Gray Sexton (Boston: Houghton Mifflin, 1981), 472. Hereafter, all of Sexton's poems are cited from this volume, even when their original publication source is identified as otherwise, and all cites appear parenthetically by page number in Gray Sexton's edition. When offering an extended analysis of any one poem, inclusive page numbers for that poem appear parenthetically in the text at the beginning of that analysis. For Dickinson's "Much Madness" see poem 435 in Johnson's *Complete Poems*.

2. Sylvia Plath, *The Collected Poems*, ed. Ted Hughes (New York: HarperCollins, 1992), 270. Hereafter, Plath's poems from this volume are cited parenthetically in the text by page number. For poems given extended analysis, the inclusive page numbers for each poem appear parenthetically at the beginning of each reading.

3. Judith Kroll, *Chapters in a Mythology: The Poetry of Sylvia Plath* (New York: Harper and Row, 1976), 211.

4. Kroll, ibid., 19; Jahan Ramazari, " 'Daddy, I Have Had to Kill You': Plath, Rage, and the Modern Elegy," *PMLA* 108, no. 5 (1993): 1142–1154; James Young, " 'I May Be a Bit of a Jew': The Holocaust Confessions of Sylvia Plath," *Philological Quarterly* 66, no. 1 (1987): 127–147; and Alicia Ostriker, *Stealing the Language: The Emergence of Women's Poetry in America* (Boston: Beacon Press, 1986), 127–128.

5. Steven Gould Axelrod, *Sylvia Plath: The Wound and Cure of Words* (Baltimore: Johns Hopkins University Press, 1990), 4–8.

6. See Mary Lynn Broe's *Protean Poetic: The Poetry of Sylvia Plath* (Columbia: University of Missouri Press, 1980), which asserts both emotional range and kinetic intensity as fundamentals of Plath's poesis.

7. Diane Middlebrook, *Anne Sexton: A Biography* (New York: Random House, 1991), 380.

8. Hume George here draws upon Maxine Kumin's own distinctions among different kinds of confessional "I"s. See Diana Hume George, *Oedipus Anne: The Poetry of Anne Sexton* (Urbana: University of Illinois Press, 1986), 96–110.

9. See Alicia Ostriker, "Anne Sexton and the Seduction of Audience," in *Sexton: Selected Criticism*, ed. Diana Hume George (Urbana: University of Illinois Press, 1988), 3–18.

10. Middlebrook, *Sexton*, 395.

11. Ralph Waldo Emerson, "The Poet," in *The Complete Works of Ralph Waldo Emerson, Volume III Essays: Second Series*, ed. Joseph Slater, Alfred Ferguson, and Jean Ferguson Carr (Cambridge, Mass.: Harvard University Press, 1983), 3–24, quote at 7.

12. Hume George, *Oedipus Anne*, xvi.

13. Anne Sexton, "Gods," from *Anne Sexton Reads Her Poetry*, recorded June 1, 1974, Caedmon Records, Inc./HarperCollins Audio, 1974.

14. Quoted in Middlebrook, *Sexton*, 42–43, 64.

15. Ibid., 65.

16. Ibid., 42.

17. Ibid., 123.

18. Margaret Homans, *Bearing the Word: Language and Female Experience in Nineteenth-Century Women's Writing* (Chicago: University of Chicago Press, 1986), 11.

19. Hume George, *Oedipus Anne*, 20.

20. Alicia Ostriker, " 'That Story': Anne Sexton and Her Transformations," in *Anne Sexton*, ed. Hume George, 263.

21. Ibid., 264.

22. See Middlebrook's reading of milk imagery in "O Ye Tounges" in *Sexton*, 353–355.

23. Ibid., 354.

24. Hume George, *Oedipus Anne*, 49.

25. Ostriker " 'That Story,' " 271.

26. Hume George, *Oedipus Anne*, 51–52. See these pages also for Hume George's speculation about possible childhood abuse by this grandfather.

27. See Middlebrook's account of Sexton's last lunch with Kumin, correcting the galleys (*Sexton*, 396).

28. Sylvia Plath, *Letters Home: Correspondence, 1950–1963*, ed. Aurelia Plath (New York: Harper and Row, 1975), 40.

29. Sylvia Plath, *The Journals of Sylvia Plath*, ed. Francis McCollough, consulting ed. Ted Hughes (New York: Dial Press, 1982), 78.

30. Sandra Gilbert, "In Yeats's House: The Death and Resurrection of Sylvia Plath," in *Coming to Light: American Women Poets in the Twentieth Century*, ed. Diane Wood Middlebrook and Marilyn Yalom (Ann Arbor: University of Michigan Press, 1985), 145–166.

31. Robert Lowell, foreword to *Ariel*, by Sylvia Plath (New York: Harper and Row, 1961).

32. Axelrod, *Plath*, 33–37.

33. Hughes asserts that much of the juvenilia selected for publication in *The Collected Poems* was written as "class assignments for her English professor at Smith College, Alfred Young Fisher" and that Plath often "followed his textual suggestions" (*Collected Poems*, ed. Hughes, 299).

34. Plath, *Letters Home*, 290.

35. Ibid., 256.

36. My thanks go to the librarians at the Mortimer Rare Book Room at Smith College for helping me to find "Song of Eve." Two typed copies of it exist there. One, which bears a campus dormitory address in the corner, apparently was written by Plath as an undergraduate and includes some handwritten comments in the margin, likely by her professor, Alfred Fisher; Ted Hughes notes that Plath wrote many poems for his workshop (*Collected Poems*, 299). Another slightly revised version bears the Elm Street address in Northampton, which suggests that Plath thought this poem deserved further work several years after her graduation from Smith.

37. Ramazari similarly characterizes Plath's "bonds" with the dead fathers of literary tradition as "strife-sealed" and asserts that by defacing the name of the dead father, rather than "revering" that name as traditional elegists do, Plath reverses "the norms of female subjugation and masculine inheritance" (" 'Daddy, I Have Had to Kill You,' " 1142–1145).

38. Axelrod characterizes Plath's relation to the canonical literary tradition as that of a "martyr" and "rebel" since she "revered men's texts" at one moment and "defaced them" the next (*Plath*, 24).

39. See Axelrod's reading of this dynamic (ibid., 25, 52–53).

40. For different perspectives on this same dynamic, see Ramazari's (" 'Daddy, I Have Had to Kill You' ") reading of melancholic mourning in "Daddy" and Susan Van Dyne's reading (*Revising Life: Sylvia Plath's Ariel Poems* [Chapel Hill: University of North Carolina Press, 1993]) of the construction of audience in the same poem.

41. This point qualifies the claims of critics who blame the erasure of the speaker on the role of language in subjecting the speaking subject. Some assumptions of psychoanalytic and postmodern theory lead some critics to overstate the phallic power of patriarchy and, to my mind, mischaracterize Plath's poetry. For example, Ramazari's assertion that Plath was "prohibited" from attaining the father's phallic

power as "all women are under patriarchy" (" 'Daddy I Have Had to Kill You,' " 1146) incredibly overlooks the fact of Plath's remarkable work. Writing is the exercise of phallic power, and key texts of Plath's foreground phallic tropes, like the "arrow" that flies into the sun, for instance, in "Ariel." On the other side of this debate about the extent of phallicism is an argument like Axelrod's for Plath's "Three Women." His utopian claim that she achieves a "language free of phallic law" (*Plath*, 168) ignores the force of patriarchal power structures.

42. See Kathleen Margaret Lant, "The Big Strip Tease: Female Bodies and Male Power in the Poetry of Sylvia Plath," *Contemporary Literature* 34, no. 4 (1993): 620–669. For example, being "inside" and "out" of a tradition may enable what Rachel Blau Duplessis has called "both/and vision" (*The Pink Guitar: Writing as Feminist Practice* [New York: Routledge, 1990], 6).

43. Van Dyne, *Revising Life*, 20–21.

44. Although readings focusing on genre, like that of the dramatic monologue I propose, are not common in Plath criticism, many critics have called for a recognition of the significance of masks and personae in her work, from Hughes to Kroll to Van Dyne. Recall that in Eliot's famous use of the form, Prufrock also uses the character of Lazarus to momentarily figure his identity.

45. Perhaps the most significant difference between Plath and the modernists is marked by her use of Holocaust tropes. While Eliot, Pound, and H.D. all engage the subject of war, Plath uses the atrocities of World War II as tropes to signify other horrors. Pound's flagrant fascism and anti-Semitism and Eliot's more subtle conservatism and anti-Semitism are well known and point to another of Plath's departures from her modernist heritage. Although many critics have criticized her use of Holocaust imagery as insensitive and inappropriate, her sympathetic identification with victims of anti-Semitic violence is clear.

46. Plath, *Letters Home*, 314.

47. Plath, *Journals*, 292.

48. Ibid., 76–77.

49. I am indebted to James Young's excellent reading of Plath's Holocaust tropes for this insight. Young argues that the Holocaust metaphor is received differently by Jewish and non-Jewish communities. He also points out that Plath's Holocaust tropes have an implic-

itly Christian frame that a Jewish writer would not be likely to use (" 'I May Be a Bit of a Jew,' " 134–144).

50. Irving Howe, quoted in Young (" 'I May Be a Bit of a Jew,' " 142).

51. Marjorie Perloff, "Icon of the Fifties," *Parnassus: Poetry in Review* 12–13, nos. 1–2 (1985): 282–285.

52. In an interview, she claimed that poetry should make personal experience "relevant to such things as Hiroshima and Dachau" (quoted in Young, " 'I May Be a Bit of a Jew,' " 135). However, elsewhere she mentions individual, psychological "concentration camps" (see Edward Butscher, *Method and Madness* [New York: Seabury Press, 1976], 335) and her desire not to swerve from depicting horrible realties, to "tell just what it's like" for the "person out of Belson—physical or physiological" (Plath, *Letters Home*, 473).

53. Gayle Wurst, " 'I've Boarded the Train There's No Getting Off': The Body as Metaphor in the Poetry of Sylvia Plath," in *Revue Francaise d'Etudes Americaines* 15, no. 44 (1990): 23–35, quote at 26.

54. See Van Dyne's *Revising Life* and Toni Saldivar's discussion of the gnostic imagination in *Sylvia Plath: Confessing the Fictive Self* (New York: Peter Lang Publishing, 1992).

55. "Dialogue *En Route*" (308–309), a sassy Adam and Eve poem that reveals both figures' egocentrism, is in Plath's juvenilia and somewhat resembles the verbal acrobatics of Marianne Moore's "Marriage."

56. Plath, *Letters Home*, 233, 276.

57. T. S. Eliot, *The Wasteland and Other Poems* (San Diego: Harcourt Brace Jovanovich, 1934), 67–70.

58. Axelrod, *Plath*, 164.

59. While Axelrod justly describes "Three Women" as one of the great poems of this century, his claim that its language is "free of phallic law" (ibid., 168) overstates the case. The prominence of the women's isolation from one another, as Pamela Annas notes (in *A Disturbance in Mirrors: The Poetry of Sylvia Plath* [Westport, Conn.: Greenwood Press, 1988], 75), emphasizes that the social context is predominantly patriarchal. The main setting, after all, is a hospital, a fundamental institution in the regulation of women's bodies in a patriarchal culture.

60. Enid Dame, *Lilith and Her Demons* (Merrick, N.Y.: Cross-Cultural Communications, 1986).

61. Rich's dialogue with Yeats occurs in a poem that takes on much of the canonical literary history and, interestingly enough, was written at almost the same historical moment as Plath's revision. Rich's "Snapshots of a Daughter-in-Law" appeared in 1963, only a year after Plath's composition of "Three Women."

62. Van Dyne's study of Plath's drafts reveals the early title of "Medusa" and suggests that it was conceived as a companion poem to "Daddy" (*Revising Life*, 93).

63. Ibid., 97.

64. As Rachel Blau Duplessis has noted, targeting Greek mythology targets the authority of classical education, while using biblical mythology appropriates an even stronger or sacred authority (*Writing Beyond the Ending: Narrative Strategies of Twentieth-Century Women Writers* [Bloomington: Indiana University Press, 1985], chap. 7).

65. Van Dyne, *Revising Life*, 96.

66. See Marjorie Perloff's "The Two Ariels: The (Re)Making of the Sylvia Plath Canon" (in *Poems in Their Place: The Intertextuality and Order of Poetic Collections*, ed. Neil Fraistat [Chapel Hill: University of North Carolina Press, 1986], 308–333) for a description of Plath's ordering of the poems and her article "Icon of the Fifties" for a sense of the unconventionality of "Morning Song" for its time.

67. As Young notes about "Mary's Song," from "Plath's Holocaust" emerges a "kind of calvary" (" 'I May Be a Bit of a Jew,' " 133).

68. Annas, *A Disturbance*, 97.

69. Plath, *Letters Home*, 468.

70. Van Dyne, *Revising Life*, 67–73.

71. Ostriker, *Stealing the Language*, 221.

72. Lant, "The Big Strip Tease," 620–669.

73. Duplessis, *Writing Beyond the Ending*, 34.

74. Van Dyne, *Revising Life*, 110.

75. Sylvia Plath, *Johnny Panic and the Bible of Dreams and Other Prose Writings* (London: Faber, 1979), 21.

76. Broe, *Protean Poetic*, 182.

77. Gilbert, "In Yeats's House," 164.

78. Van Dyne, *Revising Life*, 62.

79. Ibid., 119.

80. Kroll, *Chapters in a Mythology*, 39.

81. Ibid., 180–181.

82. Sylvia Plath, *The Bell Jar* (New York: Harper and Row, 1971), 68.

83. Perloff, "The Two Ariels," 325

84. I owe this "sighting" of the Magdalene to Alicia Ostriker's insightful reading of this manuscript in draft stage.

85. Linda Wagner-Martin notes Plath's biblical reading centered on Job in *Sylvia Plath: A Biography* (New York: Simon and Schuster, 1987), 157.

86. All biblical references are to the King James Version and are noted parenthetically.

87. Susan Van Dyne, "Fueling the Phoenix Fire: The Manuscripts of Sylvia Plath's 'Lady Lazarus,' " *Massachusetts Review: A Quarterly of Literature, Arts, and Public Affairs* 24, no. 2 (1983): 395–410, quote at 399.

88. See Axelrod, *Plath*, 101; Ostriker, *Stealing the Language*, chap. 4; and Van Dyne, *Revising Life*, chap. 1.

89. Young, " 'I May Be a Bit of a Jew,' " 128.

90. Middlebrook, *Sexton*, 355.

91. Maxine Kumin shares this detail in her introduction to Anne Sexton's *Complete Poems*, ed. Gray Sexton. The essay also appears in *Sexton: Selected Criticism*, ed. Hume George, 197–210. All references here refer to the Hume George collection.

92. Kumin, *Anne Sexton*, ed. Hume George, 197.

93. See Middlebrook, *Sexton*, 72.

94. Quoted in ibid., 201.

95. Ibid., 355

96. Kumin, *Anne Sexton*, ed. Hume George, 202.

97. Middlebrook, *Sexton*, 367.

98. Ibid., 367–368.

99. Kumin, *Anne Sexton,*ed. Hume George, 204.

100. Plath, *Journals*, 154.

101. Ibid., 259.

102. Axelrod, *Plath*, 178–180.

103. Van Dyne, *Revising Life*, 9.

104. Ibid., 8.

105. See Axelrod's reading of Hughes's appalling conduct as literary executor and his speculations about Plath's reasons for giving him the job (*Plath*, 15–20).

Chapter Three

Writing Home: The Bible and Gloria Naylor's *Bailey's Cafe* and Toni Morrison's *Song of Solomon*

"The Bible Is an Awfully Large Book"

It is a Bible-quoting battle between a frigid fundamentalist and a quasi-supernatural madam that inspires Bailey, the overarching narrator of Gloria Naylor's *Bailey's Cafe* (1992), to remark on the Bible's size.[1] "Awfully large," however, refers not merely to length. Bailey's sardonic response to the interpretive battle being waged in his cafe underlines the breadth and diversity within the ancient text that Naylor engages in her revision of several women biblical characters. With these characters, Naylor examines the constructions of heterosexual identity through which African American women's sexuality, in particular, has been understood. Safely ensconced in the "whorehouse convent" (116) that is Eve's boarding house, Esther, Jessie Bell, and two Marys tell their stories of origins. "Home" in each of the women characters' stories represents the site of the construction and control of women's identity and sexuality. Naylor's biblically informed imagination, however, constantly underscores the fact that the production of meaning is always mythical and textual as well social and historical.

Myth is equally important to Toni Morrison's novel *Song of Solomon* (1978).[2] Though the novel's title evokes the biblical

Song of Solomon just as Naylor's characters' names evoke their biblical precursors, the heart of this story belongs to another myth of origins, a folktale of flying Africans. Ancestors in this novel carry the weight and meaning of home. Milkman Dead's quest to learn about his family's past ends with his understanding of this folk song of Solomon (a.k.a. Shalimar or Sugarman) as his own story of origins. The first section of this chapter investigates the function of biblical intertexts as stories of origin in *Bailey's Cafe* before we turn to the same question in *Song of Solomon*.

Bailey's Cafe: A Mythical Home

By casting her characters as biblical figures, Naylor claims the Bible as a mythical home, a point of origin for the interpretation of gender identity in Western culture. Thus, Eve's boarding house, a way station for troubled characters, symbolizes Naylor's revisionary narrative project: *Bailey's Cafe* offers a textual halfway house between the given homes of our culture and those yet to be imagined. The architecture of this halfway house reveals three "stories," or prominent layers of signification. The first story of this new structure is founded on a critique of Genesis and some other first stories of Western culture. The second story overlays and complicates the first by rereading biblical characters with desire and claiming them as a site/cite of potential cultural change. While the first two stories overtly engage the biblical tradition as source, or original home, the third claims an alternative ontology in African American interpretive and literary traditions that provides the foundation for remaking home.[3]

Since the individual narratives of *Bailey's Cafe* all occur in the aftermath of racism, war, rape, and family dysfunction, they seem to echo Adrienne Rich's question: "In the wake of home, what would comfort be?"[4] The first woman's story, that of Sadie, a drunken prostitute sustained only by her fantasies of domestic perfection, clearly underscores the centrality of understandings of home to the tales that follow. As we saw in the poetry examined in previous chapters, the domestic scene is not the opposite of the battle front. Opening the novel with a man's story of combat in World War II suggests a connection between the violence of the war front and that of the home front. Therefore, before examining the women's narratives, we should explore the significance of war in Bailey's narrative. Whereas Plath seems to exploit Dickinson's use of war as trope for conflict with the Word of the Father, Naylor more closely resembles H.D. in her use of war as historical subject and political and literary inspiration. Both Bailey's story and the later narrative of Miss Maple, a conscientious objector, suggest that the need to come to terms with the legacy of World War II, especially as it shaped gender and racial categories, is a strong spur to Naylor's biblical revision. In crossing the space between the woman writer on the domestic front and the male combatant on the war front by creating the voice of a male soldier, Naylor echoes Gwendolyn Brooks's achievement in her sonnet cycle from 1944, "Gay Chaps at the Bar." Naylor emphasizes in Bailey's story, as Brooks's poem does, that the "bar" for African American soldiers was not just the foreign saloon or stripes of decoration, but the color bar that segregated black soldiers and even put their lives more frequently at risk than their white counterparts.

Though Bailey's civilian experience has taught him to expect this discrimination, he confesses to his wife that he realizes the war will be "the most exciting thing that ever happened in [his] life" (20–21). Here, Naylor underscores the historical gendered division of labor that assigns war as men's vocation and frequently posits it as an ultimate or formative masculine experience. Slaughtering the enemy at Guadalcanal, Bailey fights "like a man" (23). Like the World War II poets Susan Schweik surveys,[5] Naylor also analogizes the soldier's sacrifice to that of Christ. It is the possibility of resurrection, of surviving the death that surrounds him on the battlefield, however, that horrifies

Bailey: "I wasn't a coward. . . . It just became too unbearable to know I'd be doomed to come out alive. Take. This. Cross. From. Me" (26).

The twist here in perspective on both war and Christ's crucifixion as related types of male self-sacrificing heroism continues to be developed in a metaphor that substitutes the dropping of the atomic bomb for the crucifixion. In imagery evoking the apocalyptic destruction prophesied in the Book of Revelation, the "face" of destruction "gleamed brighter and its breath burned hotter than the sun" (26). The rising, swelling atomic cloud "rose like the head of a newborn," and the blood of "Hiroshima," not of Christ, is offered "in exchange" for Bailey's "soul" (26). As the comparison of the bomb cloud to a newborn's head suggests, this specter of destruction is tied to imagery of birth or resurrection, but this analogy revises the traditional reading of Christ's or the soldier's sacrifice as enabling moral life to continue. Instead, it turns back to the link between masculinity and war.

Bailey's earlier account of chants used in his combat training underlines the common use of male sexuality as a trope for violence: the question "who you gon'na fuck?" is interchangeable with the question "who you gon'na kill?" (21). As Bailey's narrating "I" expands, representing the whole destructive thrust of the bomb, it returns to imagery that again describes death in terms of sexuality but also stresses the irony of troping on a reproductive function, more logically associated with life, to represent death. His "seed rained on that city from black clouds" and "flowed with the inland tides . . . nurtured within warm currents across the curve of the earth" until it reached "a new age," finally landing in America (26). Thus, Bailey's narrative chronicles how the violence of the war front eventually comes home; as he arrives in San Francisco, he feels a "sting" as the "hard shells" of that "seed" hit land and knows that "[r]ight here on this soil, we'd be forced to watch them grow" (26). It is the horror of reaping this harvest that propels Bailey's story out of both the realism of his life in Brooklyn and the surrealism of the war and into the fantastic dimension that houses all the narratives to follow. In the extended metaphor connecting male violence to its own reproduction, Naylor also highlights the link between masculinity and war associated with the epic literary tradition. Opening the novel with Bailey's combat narrative juxtaposes the literary tradition of "arms and the man" with the biblical tradition that more overtly informs the women's stories. Furthermore, by turning Christ's crucifixion into a critique of the sacrifice of war, Bailey's narrative foreshadows the transformation in the signification of biblical language that characterizes the women's narratives. In the stories of Eve, Esther, Mary, and Jessie Bell, Naylor offers a reexamination of some of the oldest stories of our culture as the basis for revising actual and figurative homes. Rereading the Bible with the "hermeneutics of suspicion" that Bailey's story reveals, an approach that distrusts the power dynamics and traditional interpretations of the ancient text, she creates a critique powerful enough to "rupture the habits of narrative order" or "break the sentence" of some of the formative myths of Western culture.[6]

"Eve's Song" retells the Genesis narrative of Eve's creation, sin, and expulsion from the garden. Louisiana's lush and isolated delta serves as Eve's original home, but her story reveals the place to be less than Edenic even before her fall from paternal grace. Eve's adoptive parent, "Godfather," rules the miniature world of this small town with an iron fist. Like the "Burglar, Banker, Father" of Dickinson's poetry, his need for absolute control is signaled by his trinity of roles as the school's "book-keeper," the cotton exchange's "scale foreman," and the church's "preacher"; all represent his power as interpreter, measurer, and judge (85). Despite his omnipresence in the community, he is hostage to the opinion of the townsfolk, denying his adopted child physical affection just to quiet the town gossips' baseless sexual innuendo (83–84). When he discovers Eve masturbating in the fragrant "peppermint-grass" (85), Godfather sends her naked and impoverished from his home and church. While "Eve's Song" recontextualizes Eden by relocating the grand power play of myth in the petty despotism of small-town life, it also engages several fundamental interpretative issues of the ancient text.

First, "Eve's Song" makes visible an act of appropriation naturalized in Genesis: the masculine appropriation of generativity, represented in the Bible by God's sole creation of humanity and his granting of fertility to the barren wives of the patriarchs:[7]

Godfather always told me that since I never had a real mother or father and wouldn't be alive if it weren't for him, *he* would decide when I was born. . . . [W]henever I'd ask what day was my birthday, he kept changing it year to year, month to month. . . . He was patient that way, when he wanted to teach me a lesson. (82)

Godfather's insistence that he "made" Eve (90) and his refusal to reveal her birth date underscore the power dynamics of the biblical account of creation, which elides the representations of feminine dieties from the older, oral traditions it revises to establish a monotheistic creation myth.[8] "Eve's Song" thus "literalizes" the scene of creation by rewriting the romantic moment of myth as a realistic document of power struggle, simultaneously revealing and remaking the political subtext of the story of the fall. As Margaret Homans argues, this strategy of literalization, which translates the abstract figure into an "actual event or circumstance," exposes the opposition between the figurative paternal "word" and the literal but always absent maternal referent that enables the making of literary meaning. By literalizing the masculine-identified Logos of Genesis, Naylor, like the poets we examined earlier, reveals this story, which Homans calls "the modern story of language," to be a fable.[9] While the plot imitates the action of Genesis by tracing Eve's fall and expulsion, Naylor's hermeneutics of suspicion circumscribes and thus defuses the claim of biblical Logos to absolute authority. The thunder of God shrivels to Godfather's grunting in the pulpit.

The absence of Adam and Lucifer in Naylor's version also exposes her own interpretive investment in the myth. If John Milton explains "God's ways to man" in *Paradise Lost*, Naylor examines the significance of Genesis to women in *Bailey's Cafe*. By stripping Eve's story of both her mate and Satan, Naylor exposes the layer of the ancient myth that establishes the relationship of the foremother to paternal authority. Exiled from Godfather's realm, she is literally far removed from the Law of the Father, though she carries the Father's Word inscribed within her. Thus, Naylor's retelling of Eve's fall and exile allegorizes the genesis of women writers' authority on the margins of paternal law.

Another aspect of Naylor's "literalization" of Genesis targets not the text, but its popular construction and reception. Eve's sin has become synonymous in popular culture with sexuality, although that depends upon a perverse reading of the text that clearly defines her disobedience as consuming the fruit of the knowledge of good and evil. Naylor's recasting of Eve's crime as masturbation reveals the popular conflation of sin with sexuality and decriminalizes this original "sin" as the innocent sexual self-exploration of a lonely adolescent.

If "Eve's Song" debunks the myth of an original Edenic home by confronting the sexualization of Eve's sin, the story of "Sweet Esther" debunks the myth of the sexual power of the enslaved woman.[10] Like the biblical Esther, the enslaved Hebrew princess who liberates her people by pleasing her captor king, Naylor's Esther feels like a "princess" in the relative opulence of her new home (96). Amid the luxuries of fine china and a bed "trimmed with lace," the twelve-year-old "bride" does not immediately realize she has been sold by her brother to satisfy the sadistic sexuality of a wealthy farmer. Once she is able to name what they do in the cellar as "making evil," she buys her own body back by fulfilling her brother's bargain: for twelve years of her brother's food and board, she surrenders twelve years to the sadist's cellar (98–99). Unlike her biblical namesake, Esther can never secure the liberty of others, although she eventually finds refuge for herself in Eve's house. She considers murdering her torturer to spare "the other young girls waiting in line to sleep along in his pink-and-lace bed. The other girls with brothers." But she realizes that there "are just too many of them to kill. And there are just too many twelve-year-olds" (99).

Just as "Eve's Song" allegorizes the marginalized writer's relation to the original home, center, or source of authority, "Sweet Esther" allegorizes the crime of slavery in the cellar of American culture. As Naylor brings us into Esther's consciousness, we hear the dehumanizing labels that echo in her memory: "The black gal. Monkey Face. Tar. Coal. Ugly. Soot" (95). Though this story is set in the early twentieth century, the "black gal" remains an object of exchange between men and subject to the will of her master. Thus, Esther's body evokes "the captive body" that Hortense Spillers argues "becomes a source of an irresistible, destructive sexuality"[11] and a site for porno-troping as Esther and her owner "make evil" in the basement. This revision of Esther's story not only debunks the myth of the sexually powerful slave, it also figures the repression of such scenes of abuse. Esther's attempt to articulate her experience is haunted by echoes of the command "We won't speak about this, Esther" (95–99). In sum, the unspeakability of Esther's abuse evokes the unspeakability of the sexual violations of enslaved women and the legacy of slavery on constructions of African American women's sexuality.

In the stories immediately following Esther's, Naylor articulates another repressed aspect of representations of sexuality: the construction of the virgin/whore dichotomy. In "Mary: (Take One)," the name "Mary" signifies both the Virgin and Mary Magdalene. By collapsing these two into one character, Naylor's hermeneutics of suspicion here reveals how the identities of "virgin" and "whore," though often understood as essences, are socially constructed and mutually defining.

When the gorgeous Mary (a.k.a. Peaches) enters Bailey's Cafe, a local pimp, Sugar Man, whispers what "every man" was thinking: she is "born to be fucked" (102). Despite her doting father's attempt to protect her by dressing her in Mary blue and even building a brick wall around their house, Mary ultimately fulfills the social script to which Sugar Man refers. Naylor's critique of this script, however, shifts the moment when the whore is revealed from the act of sexual intercourse to the act of gazing:

Everywhere I turned I could see her. But what was she doing in my room? She was a whore and I was Daddy's baby. Every mirror outside told me what she was: the brown mirrors, hazel mirrors, blue mirrors, oval, round, and lashed mirrors of all their eyes when they looked at me. (104)

Seeing the reflection of the "whore" rather than "Daddy's baby" in the eyes of her community radically destabilizes Mary's self-perception, her internal eye/I. Daddy's favorite child ultimately splits her identity to accommodate the sexualized self that the suspicious social mirrors reflect. Naylor's metaphor also suggests that Mary's original identity as the virginal Peaches was no more true or essential than the "whore" she later becomes, since her father's devotion to her also reflects the larger culture's racist fascination for lighter skin: as his wife laments, he is "color-struck" (102). Thus, the early love and security Mary felt in her father's brick-fenced home was merely the first mirror-trick, since it too reflected who she resembled, rather than who she was. Mary concludes that only if she "had been born into a world without mirrors" might there "have been a chance for a real home" (108).

The dream of a "real home," however, does not necessarily posit the existence of an identity previous to or entirely independent of social context. Rather, Mary's dilemma points to a gendered twist or additional layer to W. E. B. Du Bois's definition of racial double-consciousness as the "sense of always looking at one's self through the eyes of others."[12] A phrase Mary has heard since childhood—"that gal's got promise"— further reveals how the split between the virgin and the whore

in her identity signifies no lost whole self, but the establishment of identity through social negotiations (104). "Promise,"
her potential value on the marriage or sexual market, implies
not only value *to* someone, but also value *for* something and
thus provides the basis of a contract:

in my mirrors I would try to see what she had promised them that
would cause the heat to seep up through the rough denim of their
pant legs. . . . What have you promised them? I whisper to her.—You.
You. You. (104).

At last, Mary's eye/I recognizes the "you" in the mirror as the
whore who contracted this promise. With this depiction of the
ability of the "promise" to organize Mary's identity, Naylor
demonstrates how such social negotiations actually constitute
the individuals they purport to regulate.[13] In short, by demon-
strating that whores are made, not born, Naylor ironizes Sugar
Man's initial comment that Mary is "born to be fucked." As
Mary's "I" fulfills the contract by surrendering her "you," her
position as exchanger, rather than merely the object of exchange,
frees her by chasing the "demon" from her "mirror" (105).

This liberation, nevertheless, is only temporary because the
bifurcated self inevitably collapses into the singular somatic
self; in other words, Mary may have two minds, but she has
only one body. Mary's disgust for the "whore" turns to self-
loathing when "very slowly over time" she realizes that she "actually enjoyed being held and touched" (107). Thus, Mary's
story demonstrates how the virgin/whore dichotomy rein-
forces the essentialist assumptions behind the pattern of blam-
ing female victims. Formerly, Mary knew that the "you" in the
mirror "had always been a whore," but now she thinks, "I was
probably always asking for it" (107).

Since the contract has lost its power to maintain the split between virgin and whore in Mary's identity, she has to attack the
force that gave the lie to that split—her own body. Smiling into
the bathroom mirror, Mary destroys her reflection by cutting

her face with a beer opener. This marking of her own body is an attempt to rewrite the implications of the virgin/whore script as she literally dis-figures herself. Eve alone recognizes Mary's design: "only the scar" is "reflected" in Eve's eyes when she pronounces Mary beautiful.

Jessie Bell's story immediately follows Mary's and further explores the difficulty of rewriting the cultural scripts of sexuality, particularly African American women's sexuality. While the hermeneutics of suspicion denaturalizes the virgin/whore dichotomy by tracing the social construction of the identity of the whore in Mary's story, it denies the label altogether in Jessie's. Although she bears the ill fame of the biblical Jezebel, Jessie's sexual relations with her husband and female lover offer one of the novel's rare representations of mutuality and choice. By the novel's close, the sexually infamous Jessie is known especially for her virginal refusal of "gentlemen callers" at Eve's "whorehouse convent" (117).

Like the biblical Jezebel, Jessie enters unfamiliar territory when she becomes associated with a king. Naylor transforms the power of the biblical King Ahab into the political dabbling of a socially prominent African American family, the "Kings." Like the queen from Sidon, Jessie is a foreigner to the Kings' world; the crux of her difference here, however, is not ethnicity or nationality, but class. Naylor reconfigures Jezebel's sabotage of Israelite politics as Jessie Bell's resistance to the self-loathing social politics of the Kings. Like the biblical queen's persistent loyalty to the Canaanite gods of her people, Jessie maintains the integrity of her social roots and refuses to adopt what she calls the Kings' "religion": "White folks . . . were Uncle Eli's god. And it was a god I wasn't buying" (125).

Conservative elders in the King family, like Uncle Eli, never accept the iconoclastic girl from the docks, and their discouragement contributes to her divorce and disgrace when her drug abuse and long-term affair with a woman become public. If mirrors symbolize the forces blocking Mary's attempts to establish a real home, the papers or the press symbolize the source of the destruction of Jessie's home. As she notes, she has "no friends putting out *The Herald Tribune*. And it's all about who's in charge of keeping the records" (118). Both Mary's social mirrors and Jessie's bad press represent the importance of naming, even as Naylor's engagement of the Bible and the cultural scripts of women's sexuality alter the signification of those names.

Furthermore, the construction of Jessie as a jezebel reveals that the homes of origins in all of these tales are founded implicitly on heterosexual assumptions. While the white-worshipping elder King uncle never liked Jessie's independence, her fall as Jezebel comes about only after her arrest in a raid of a "dyke club" (131). For years, Jessie refused her husband's offer to welcome her "special friend" to their house, reasoning that "my needs were my own. But so was my home" (125). By implicitly defining her relationships with women as "not home," she locates her lesbianism literally on the side. With this representation of an alternative sexuality located outside the home, Naylor marks the function of the traditional family home to represent the boundaries of sexual identity. This is more readily apparent when the issue of Jessie's identity is seen as part of Naylor's larger pattern of reconfiguring conflicting identities by figuring them within a single individual. We have seen the formative war between the virgin and the whore in the construction of Mary's identity in "Mary: (Take One)." Similarly, in the novel's closing story, "Mary: (Take Two)," identity categories again fuse within a single person. There, it is not sexuality, but race and ethnicity that are the locus of redefinition, as Mariam, an Ethiopian Jew, is driven from her home. Jessie Bell's caring, consensual relationships with her husband and her female lover offer the novel's only depiction of an adult sexuality free from coercion or prostitution, yet she too is driven from her home. By fusing the homosexual and heterosexual in Jessie Bell's character, virgin and whore in Mary's, and black and Jew in Mariam's, Naylor questions the traditional construction and opposition of these pairs of identity categories.

When Jessie can no longer maintain a public/private split in her sexual identity, she lands in "the women's house of detention," where Eve eventually leaves her calling card. In addition to the address, however, Jessie, like all of Eve's boarders, must know what she calls the "delta dust" to enter her sanctuary. It is this knowledge that calls forth the second story, or layer of signification, in this novel's engagement of the Bible.

In Eve's thousand-year journey from Godfather's home, she literally finds new grounds for her identity in the lush lands of the delta. "The delta dust exists," she discovers, "to grow things, anything in soil so fertile its tomatoes, beans, and cotton are obscene in their richness" (90). In her own time of dryness and exile, the dust permeates her very pores, preserving and resculpting her.

Layers and layers of it were forming, forming, doing what it existed to do, growing the only thing it could find in one of the driest winters in living memory. Godfather always said that he made me, but I was born of the delta. (90)

As an alternative agent of creation to the formative Logos of Genesis, the delta dust symbolizes the creative impulse that constructs the second story or way of remaking meaning in the halfway house that is Naylor's novel. If the first story rereads some of the founding narratives of our culture with suspicion, the second story permeates them with a fertile and enlivening desire, just as the delta dust remakes Eve.

As Alicia Ostriker has shown, reading the Bible with a hermeneutics of desire as well as a hermeneutics of suspicion allows the revisionist writer "to insert herself into the story by identifying its spiritualities with her sensualities, and by feminizings of the divine."[14] The resulting expansion of possible biblical interpretations leads in *Bailey's Cafe* to a postmodern foregrounding of the traditionally subterranean process of making meaning. In other words, the halfway house of Naylor's fiction always presents itself as a made thing, attempting not to authorize one biblical interpretation, but to dislocate any single or unitary truth as the object of interpretation. Furthermore, Naylor's postmodern approach to the ancient texts of the Bible invites readers to similarly open up her own work. *Bailey's Cafe*, in fact, operates as what Karla Holloway has called a "plurisignant" text, in which constantly shifting meanings can be located only on a "threshold," rather than formulated definitively in some "rigid structure."[15] It is this plurality of possible meanings, the very open-ended quality of Naylor's imagination, that finds in Eve traces of a divine foremother.

Eve's assertion that she was "born of the delta" rather than "made" by Godfather reverses the original masculine appropriation of generativity exposed by Naylor's rereading of Genesis in "Eve's Song." Remade by the delta, Eve represents an earth mother, evoking the Near Eastern tradition of fertility goddesses, which were written out of the creation myths when the redactors of Genesis revised ancient and diverse oral traditions. Naylor's reimagination of Eve represents a resurgence of the feminine divine repressed in the Bible.[16] As if in revenge for the repression of the feminine, Eve's re-created Garden of Eden at her boarding house features a mutilated tree at its center. This castrated "stump" is encircled year-round by flowers worthy of Georgia O'Keeffe's brush, and Eve makes these lush lilies, traditionally associated with female sexuality, bloom in and out of season.

Beyond her extraordinary gardening ability and thousand-year life span, several other aspects of Eve's character mark her as a female figure of the divine. Her refusal to justify herself, asserting that beyond "good or bad or what I am—I am" (85), echoes God's paradoxical self-description, "I Am That I Am" (Exodus 3.14). Moreover, like Christ, she heals the afflicted, promising Mary's distraught father to one day return her to him "whole" (113). Similarly, she proves herself to be Jessie's savior by forcing her to confront her own demons (136). Despite her healing powers and compassion, Eve maintains a divine detachment that spurs Jessie to call her an "icy, icy Mama"

(118). The strongest evidence of Eve's power, however, is to be found not in her deeds, but in her voice.

In several chapters of *Bailey's Cafe*, italicized passages embedded in the character's own narration represent his or her internal voice.[17] These interior monologues provide insight into the characters' motivations and understandings of their own identities and histories. In sum, these stream-of-consciousness interludes offer themselves as keys to unlocking the character's identity. Near the conclusion of Jessie Bell's story, Eve's interior monologue surfaces with the prophetic authority of the Bible itself (136).

This episode begins with a battle of biblical quotations that dramatizes conflicting approaches to interpretation. Sister Carrie, a hypocritical Bible-thumper, takes some poetic license with a few of her favorite passages condemning Jessie's "vile affections" (134). Bailey notes that to hear Sister Carrie, "you'd think loose women were the only thing ever on the Lord's mind" and that Eve, Carrie's archenemy, can match her quote for quote, citing chapter and verse with flawless precision (134). Yet, after Eve seals her victory by reciting Ezekiel's condemnation of hypocritical "sisters," one more biblical recitation appears in the scene. Unlike the other appearances of biblical texts, this one does not offer itself as a quotation referring to the Bible, but as an interior monologue referring to Eve.

Glossing Eve's healing of Jessie's addiction, the voice asserts that

when I passed by thee, and saw thee polluted in thine own blood . . . I said, Live; yea, I said unto thee when thou was in thy blood, Live. (136)

Indented and italicized like the interior voices of other characters, this interlude offers not another recitation of a biblical text, but a re-citation or relocation of voice and authority. With these words, the prophet Ezekiel describes his resuscitation and nurturance of Jerusalem, the city of God so often described in the Old Testament as unfaithful or as a whore.[18] This passage, which simultaneously evokes the biblical prophet and Naylor's Eve, functions as what Mikhail Bakhtin has termed a "hybrid construction," a seemingly unitary utterance that actually contains "two 'languages,' two semantic and axiological belief systems."[19] The indentation and italicization of this passage serve as the "compositional markers" that, as Bakhtin asserts, attribute the utterance to a "single speaker" yet highlight the dual reference of the words marked. Thus, this interior monologue is fundamentally dialogic in nature since the Word here, fusing Ezekiel and Eve, simultaneously presents both the authoritative discourse of the Bible and what Bakhtin calls the "internally persuasive word."[20] In short, the authority of biblical Logos is inseparable from the authority of Eve's voice here.

Naylor's construction of Eve's voice in this passage epitomizes her larger, transformative revision of biblical texts through the hermeneutics of desire; in sum, this passage marks Naylor's reversal of the process of exile and her reclamation of home. Furthermore, Eve's voice here concretizes and represents the signifying practice Naylor has deployed throughout. By recontextualizing biblical texts in the stories of Eve, Esther, Mary, and Jessie Bell, Naylor dialogues with biblical myth, revises it, and gives voice to significations that have not been heard before. The transgression implicit in this shift in authority is dramatized in one of the final scenes of *Bailey's Cafe*.

The mother of Mariam, the miraculously pregnant and mildly retarded virgin exiled from her strictly orthodox Jewish Ethiopian community, enters the holy space forbidden to women in order to pray for her daughter. Her resolve not "to bargain with God" or "plead her goodness" mirrors this novel's insistence on dialogue with the Bible. Naylor's text, like Mariam's mother's prayer, demands "pure and simple justice" (156). Yet the conclusion of this scene reflects the fear that accompanies this bold assertion of authority. The crowd of worshippers, shocked and disoriented by Mariam's mother's daring, push her over the "threshold . . . of no return"; she falls on the "sacrificial altar" and immediately "turns to stone"

(157). Mariam's mother's fate, like that of Lot's wife, represents the punishment that many women fear if they claim title to a portion of sacred ground, if they refuse to remain in exile. Significantly, Mariam herself dies soon after giving birth due to a failure of imagination, literally drowning in the flood of her own faulty mental conjuring (228).

Mariam's story, however, also evidences authorial daring along with fear by dramatizing Naylor's revisionist project in her attempt to bear the Word differently. Mariam's narrative, "Mary: (Take Two)," offers another scene like that of "Eve's Song" where the abstract and figurative is literalized. While this strategy in "Eve's Song" produces an allegory of the genesis of the woman writer's authority in exile, the revision of the Virgin birth offers an allegory of one woman writer's own reproduction and delivery of meaning. The child born to Mariam represents the "Word, the embodiment of Logos," but his character, once again, offers a Bakhtinian hybrid construction.[21]

The miraculous infant inevitably refers to Christ and thus claims a textual origin or home in the Gospels. However, by sending baby George to Irene Jackson's shelter, Naylor links the ending of this novel to the beginning of the story line of her earlier work *Mama Day*. By claiming a previous novel as another textual source or home, Naylor rocks this baby in the cradle of her own fictional world. The identity of the miraculous infant is constructed between two frames of reference: the biblical Word and Naylor's word. While George's birth concludes *Bailey's Cafe* by marking the sad fact that some children are "brought fourth in limbo" (227), Naylor's use of this "child of light" to weave together her own novels celebrates the potential of narrative to construct an imaginative alternative, or refuge from perpetual liminality. This final signification on a (pre)text that she herself has authored only marks the larger reconstructive process of the whole novel. Balancing suspicion of the traditional use of the Bible in representations of women's sexuality with an enlivening desire to rewrite the Word in her own image, Naylor creates a text that, like the back door of

Bailey's Cafe, opens into possibility. By claiming textual homes in the Bible and in African American discursive tradition, *Bailey's Cafe* reformulates both and demonstrates the long process of remaking home.

The Song of Solomon and the Song of Morrison

Toni Morrison's *Song of Solomon* functions as an important antecedent for Naylor's *Bailey's Cafe*. Published in 1978, fourteen years before Naylor's novel, *Song of Solomon* similarly engages the Bible through its title and biblically named characters and simultaneously engages African American expressive tradition through the myth of the flying Africans. Critics have offered only occasional and tentative ruminations about the intertextual question that the title begs. What does this tale of love and murder, this quest for family history and identity, have to do with the biblical Song of Solomon? To some, the centrality of the myth of the flying Africans to Morrison's novel entirely redirects the reference of the title, pointing to the novel's origins in African rather than biblical myth. The brilliance of the novel, however, truly derives from its ability to bring the two precursor texts into dialogue, to make them speak with one voice that is unique to Morrison's text—in short, to form another example of the hybrid construction that inspirits Naylor's novel. While Morrison's use of African myth is as obvious and key a structural component of this work as Naylor's use of blues is in her novel, the use of biblical myth in *Song of Solomon* is a subtle lesson in reading and misreading.

A seemingly minor scriptural reference offers an important clue to interpreting the role of the biblical Song of Songs in this novel. Brenda Marshall points out that when Pilate, a quasi-supernatural central character, performs a "mammy" act for the police, she misquotes Matthew 21.2.[22] Humbling herself to win the release of her nephew and his pal, Pilate explains to the police that the sack the boys stole from her contains the bones of her husband, "Mr. Solomon" (207). She kept them near her because as "the Bible say what so e're the Lord hath brought together, let no man put asunder—Matthew Twenty-one:Two" (207). As Marshall notes, statements about the union of man and wife are actually found in Matthew 19.6 and Mark 10.9. This misquotation, then, is really Pilate's sly joke on the boys who have robbed her and the police who require her self-abasement.[23] In Matthew 21.2, Jesus instructs his disciples to "go into the village" and find "an ass and a colt tied" and "loose them." In their jail cell, Milkman, Pilate's nephew, and his friend, Guitar, certainly resemble the ass and the colt that need liberation, so Pilate's misquotation actually offers a coded but pertinent application of the Gospels. This scene represents a minilesson in biblical interpretation that is repeated on a larger scale in the novel's reference to the Song of Solomon.

Pilate misquotes a sacred song from her family's history in an equally significant way. Throughout the story, she sings of "Sugarman," who has flown away, who has "cut across the sky" and "gone home" (6). We learn that Sugarman actually is a flawed remembrance of "Solomon," but even her act of singing results from misinterpretation. When the ghost of her murdered father repeatedly says "sing" to her, it seems as if he is urging her to lift her voice. What Pilate assumes to be a verb, however, is really a noun: her father is calling out Pilate's own mother's name, "Sing." Pilate never knew her Native American mother, Singing Byrd, who died while delivering her. Pilate is similarly cut off from her larger family history, including the full story of the Sugarman about whom she sings. When Milkman, the novel's protagonist, travels to the area of Pilate's childhood and discovers his family's history preserved in place names and children's games, he realizes that Pilate's Sugarman is a bastardized form of the name of the area's legendary figure and its ancestor, Solomon. According to local lore, Solomon escaped slavery by flying back to Africa. In the novel's penultimate scene, Milkman shares his discoveries about their family history with Pilate: the bones she has carried all these years are actually the bones of her own father who longs to be buried near his wife, Sing (333). Thus, Pilate's lie to the police, that she was carrying her husband's, Mr. Solomon's, bones in her sack, was closer to the truth than she knew; she was actually carrying her father's, Jake Solomon's bones. The song of Sugarman or Solomon is really the song of her ancestors.

The reader's enlightenment follows Pilate's own path to understanding. Just as Pilate learns of her misreading of her family's history, we come to understand our misreading of the novel's title. With biblically named characters like Pilate, Ruth, Corinthians and Magdalene, readers may first assume the novel's title also refers to the biblical Song of Solomon. But Milkman's discovery of the myth of flying Africans, his own family's song of Solomon, redirects the reference of the title to an African myth by the conclusion of the novel. The biblical reference of the title therefore appears to be a red herring, a device that simply delays our encounter with the African mythic precursor of this story. I would contend, however, that the hermeneutical lesson here is even more complicated. Just as Pilate's misquoting of the Gospels to the police actually offers an acute commentary on the situation, so the faulty reference to the biblical Song of Songs offers deeper commentary on some primary thematic and structural issues in the novel.

As one of the finest and most famous love songs in English literature, the intertextuality of the Bible's Song of Solomon with Morrison's novel underscores the thematic centrality of love in *Song of Solomon*. While Morrison's story of racial oppression, murder, and dysfunctional families may not appear to be a love song at first glance, "love has no uncomplicated hymns," as Anne Sexton has noted. For readers unfamiliar with the Song of Solomon, a brief description may be helpful.

Commentators on the biblical book, often referred to fondly as "the Song," universally focus on the love between the Shulamite maiden and her "beloved." The first link between the biblical Song and Morrison's novel is the ambivalent reference of both works' titles. We have seen how the novel's title points to both biblical and African mythic precursors. The "of" in the biblical title is also ambivalent; the Song has been read as "of Solomon" (that is, written by the ancient king) and sometimes as "to Solomon" (that is, addressed to Solomon as the famous beloved). Past interpreters tended to make the powerful sensuality of the Song palatable to the pious by reading it as an allegory of Christ's love for the church. More recent commentators, however, have read it more literally as a celebration of erotic human love. Phyllis Trible, for instance, analyzes this "symphony of love" as a redress or fulfillment of the potential inherent in the first couple's love that went awry in the Garden of Eden.[24] The lover's union, like that of Adam and Eve, indeed takes place in an Edenic garden. The landscape of the Song is sometimes a setting for the search for the beloved and their lovemaking and sometimes a metaphor for the sensuality of their play and union. This "enchanting interfusion between the literal and metaphoric realms" stands alone in the Bible, according to Robert Alter, as the only place where "the gratification of love" is celebrated though "all five senses of the subject."[25]

Only one erotic relationship in Morrison's *Song of Solomon* can be described as approaching this type of physical and emotional joy of love. Nearing the end of his quest, Milkman finds pleasure, acceptance, and his own capacity for truly respecting a woman in his idyllic encounter with Sweet. The uncomplicated sweetness of their lovemaking, however, stands in sharp contrast to the novel's other loves, which are all burdened by economic, racial, or gender oppression. Powerful, if warped, love thematically unites the novel's disparate characters. For example, Milkman's mother, Ruth, loves him as "a passion" but never as "a separate real person," just as she never fully separated from her father (131). The warping of love in dysfunctional families is mirrored on a grander scale in the passionate motivation of the Seven Days, a group of seven black men who murder random whites to revenge murders of their own race. Guitar, Milkman's best friend and a member of the Seven Days, explains to him, it "ain't about hating white people. It's about loving us. About loving you. My whole life is love" (159).

Another group member, Porter, shouts the same message to the women of his community as he drunkenly threatens suicide: "Don't you see I love ya? I'd die for ya, kill for ya. I'm saying I love ya . . . God have mercy" (26). Pilate too begs for "mercy" at the funeral of her granddaughter, Hagar, who has died of lovesickness. Furious at her inability to protect her "baby girl" from her self-destructive obsession with Milkman, Pilate rages over her casket, "And she was *loved!*" (319).

Clearly, Morrison's love song departs drastically from the blissful, erotic union of the Song of Songs. It is as if the intensity of the biblical lovers' passion is dispersed throughout an entire community and twisted by the troubles that shape these people's lives. This revision of the theme of love indicates the productivity of the hermeneutics of suspicion in Morrison's reading of the Song of Songs. As we have seen with writers from Dickinson to Plath to Naylor, this hermeneutic refuses the "given" of the biblical text. The world of Morrison's novel was never an idyllic garden, "without the urgent context of history and nationhood," as one critic has described the biblical Song.[26] American history, particularly the continuing impact of centuries of slavery, racism, and sexism, is the fulcrum of critique that inspires Morrison's biblical revision. Perhaps Morrison's novel sets out to reveal what happens to the human potential for love in a world where a black father is shot off a fence for trying to protect the land he cultivated, where his son evicts widows from his own community in his obsession to protect property, and where "four little colored girls" are bombed in church (173). Summing up the significance of historical location, Guitar tells Milkman, "Goddam . . . I do believe my whole life's geography" (114). Similarly, the Shulamite maiden's sigh "I am sick of love" becomes in a misogynist world the lovesickness of "doormat women" like Hagar, who have no sense of self-worth beyond their sexual attractiveness (Song of Solomon 2.5; *Song of Solomon* 308). In sum, the cultural, historical location of the force of love makes all the difference in Morrison's love song.

Yet, as in the other examples of biblical revision we have examined, Morrison's text also resonates sympathetically with its biblical precursor. Several issues point to the presence of the hermeneutics of desire, which identifies with the earlier text, as well as the hermeneutics of suspicion in Morrison's revision. Guitar, of all people, voices a vision of love without domination as he attempts to convince Hagar to abandon her possessive love of Milkman:

> It's a bad word, "belong." Especially when you put it with somebody you love. . . . Did you ever see the way clouds love a mountain? They circle all around it . . . with nothing to hide him or bind him. (306)

Though Guitar's metaphoric definition of love recalls the equality and mutuality of most of the Song of Songs, love in the biblical Song is, at least briefly, complicated by oppression. Morrison's insistence of the importance of "geography" may in fact expand on a moment when history intrudes upon the lovers' idyll.

Although some readers brush aside the Shulamite's account of the brutality of the "watchmen" as a dream sequence or a necessary counterpoint to the sweetness of love, it tears the otherwise seamless fabric of the love song.[27] The maiden recounts how her search for the beloved is interrupted:

> the watchmen that went about the city found me,
> they smote me; they wounded me;
> the keepers of the walls took away
> my veil from me. (5.7)

As Ostriker argues, this scene should "awaken our longing for justice" for women who in ancient and contemporary times risk bodily harm when they venture onto the streets alone at night or dare to pray at the sacred wall.[28] But an even more significant resonance of the *Song of Solomon* with the biblical Song derives not from the maiden's moment of vulnerability, but from her power. The strength of her presence parallels Pilate's strength in some vital ways.

The Song of Songs departs from much of the Bible not only in its erotic content, but also in the fact that it is sung by a woman. Although the Shulamite maiden and her beloved both speak, her voice opens and closes the text and is generally heard as the "most prominent."[29] The strength of her voice, for many readers of the Song, both enables and illuminates the mutuality of her relationship with her beloved. Though Milkman, the misguided main character of Morrison's text, only begins to aspire to such a love at the end of his journey, his aunt Pilate has always had the ability to command equality and the expansive soul to love without reservation. Perhaps the Shulamite functions in some ways as a precursor to Pilate. After all, Pilate toils in the vineyards, like the Shulamite maiden, for her trade as a wine maker. Like the Shulamite, she too is "black" and "comely," though her power to attract derives more from her stature and strength than from aesthetically perfect features. Could the perpetual wine-stain purple of Pilate's lips signify a textual residue of the desire expressed in the Song: "Let him kiss me with the kisses of his mouth: for thy love is better than wine" (Song 1.2)? Pilate's "alien's gift for compassion" and ability to "teach" what is needed not for "this world" but for the "next" indeed suggests that her spirit has been divinely kissed (55).

Even the biblical reference of her name, though, is once again a lesson in misreading. Feeling abandoned by God, her illiterate father selects the name "Pilate" from the Bible for the shape of its letters, like a "princely" and "protective" "tree" (18). While Pilate's character is the opposite of the betraying biblical Pilate, she does live up to her father's interpretation of the Word by providing shelter to her whole family. Her character, furthermore, reverberates off other biblical figures unsuggested by her name. Born without a navel, she recalls Eve. But she also recalls Christ as she takes a bullet for Milkman and voices her agape love for humanity: "I wish I'd a knowed more people. I would of loved 'em all" (336). Pilate's love is not as strong as death—she gives up the ghost in Milkman's arms. The novel's conclusion, however, structurally replicates the famous assertion from the last chapter of the Song:

> Set me as a seal upon thine heart,
> as a seal upon thine arm:
> for love is strong as death. (8.6)

My students often puzzle over the ambiguous ending of *Song of Solomon*. The novel closes with Milkman, who has always yearned for flight, poised in midair. He is leaping either into his new life, which will be sustained by what he has learned about his history and the nature of love, or to his death in "the killing arms of his brother," Guitar. I have wondered along with my students why, after we have accompanied Milkman on his long quest, are we not permitted to know of his death or his survival? This crucial moment, however, is also suspended in the ancient text. Despite the Song's display and celebration of eros, the maiden refuses to make supernatural claims for love's power: it is not stronger than death. Thus, we cannot witness Milkman's miraculous survival. Death, however, is also not stronger than love. Thus, we cannot witness Milkman's likely demise. Love and death must hold each other in place, balanced on either side of the immortal equation: "love is strong as death." As Milkman leaps off of the rock from which his ancestor, Solomon, took flight, Morrison's novel also takes flight from its mythic bedrock. In this moment, both the African myth of the flying Solomon tribe and the biblical Song of Solomon come together. Responding to a dual heritage of biblical myth and African lore, what this novel truly offers is a uniquely layered Song of Morrison.

"Betwixt and Between": Father Blues, Mother Hurston, and the Word

The biblical revision witnessed by both Naylor's and Morrison's novels is inseparable from an alternative literary and cul-

tural tradition very different from the traditions engaged by
the writers examined in earlier chapters. The discourses of psy-
choanlaysis and the Western literary canon are paramount in
the works of H.D., Plath, and Sexton. However, Morrison and
Naylor, as participants in the late-twentieth-century renaissance in African American women's writing, have available to
them the oral traditions of African mythology, the blues, and
the African American literary tradition. As Morrison has said
about her own writing and black fiction in general, the "presence of the ancestor" is very important.[30] And this literary ancestor may foster and shape biblical revision like the intimate
audiences did for the poets we examined earlier.

For instance, an epigraph in *Bailey's Cafe* evokes the blues, a
musical form invented by African Americans, as both muse and
medium of Naylor's creation:

> the blues open
> a place never
> closing:
> Bailey's Cafe

Each character's blues song is orchestrated as part of a larger
performance including the "vamp," the "jam," and the "wrap."
While authors frequently metaphorize their work as music or
the act of writing as singing, the blues offers a particularly apt
metaphor for Naylor's narrative strategies. What better
medium could there be for this narrative halfway house of
"folks . . . in transition" (219) than the blues, which Houston
Baker characterizes as a "scene of arrivals and departures," a
"juncture," a "place betwixt and between"?[31]

But more significant than the stylistic or thematic parallels
between Naylor's storytelling and the blues is the function of
the blues as a "matrix" or "womb" of African American culture.[32] As such, the blues tradition offers an alternative ontology, a discursive point of origin, that, unlike the authorizing
Logos of Genesis, is uniquely African American. Essentially

oral and communal, the blues, furthermore, is akin to the African American tradition of storytelling, which provides an alternative base for authority to the informing Logos of the white male tradition.[33] Like the musical tradition of the blues, the African American literary tradition of the "speakerly" text provides an alternative discursive point of origin for both Morrison's and Naylor's novels.[34] For example, hearing the stories of the characters who frequent *Bailey's Cafe* in their own voices simultaneously underscores the singularity of each individual's history and the choral effect of reiterated themes, just as the communal or "neighborhood" voices do in *Song of Solomon*.[35] However, the use of this tradition of voice in *Bailey's Cafe*, like the use of biblical tradition, works toward disintegration and cacophony as often as it does toward integration and harmony. This dissonance, furthermore, represents another manifestation of African American literary tradition.

Karla Holloway asserts that "voice" in literature by African American women is "manipulated—inverted from its usual dimension and re-placed into non-traditional spheres (layers) of the text."[36] While this technique causes some "dislocation" of meaning, as evidenced by the indeterminacy of interpretation in Morrison's and Naylor's biblical revisions, the "thematic emphasis on the recovery of some dimension of voice" balances the "dispersion" of voice.[37] Milkman, for example, clearly recovers a sense of identity when he discovers that Pilate's song narrates his ancestry. Similarly for Mary in *Bailey's Cafe*, the deconstruction of the virgin/whore dichotomy dislocates the interpretation of the gospel's two Marys, but it enables Naylor's character's assertion of voice, as evidenced by Mary's marking or rewriting of her body. Thus, the conflicting tendencies of these novelists' biblical revision, driven by both suspicion and desire, finally articulate an authoritative, if complicatedly intertextual, voice. The shape of this voice, which we defined earlier as a "hybrid construction," is undoubtedly influenced by the oral traditions of African American biblical interpretation.

Both the hermeneutics of suspicion and desire take a very de-
cided shape when seen in the context of American slavery. The
Bible, after all, was used as a tool in the domination of enslaved
people, and ministers frequently dwelt on passages exhorting
slaves' obedience. Yet enslaved people combated such sermoniz-
ing with the strength of their own "faith assertions" that led
them to "reject any teaching" that used the gospel to justify slavery.[38] Renita Weems also argues that the black church focused on
texts that corroborated its people's own sense of identity, their
"values and yearnings." Furthermore, the criminalization of lit-
eracy required the oral circulation of biblical stories, which implicitly discouraged the storyteller's "allegiance to any official
text, translation, or interpretation."[39] Both novels, however, are
not only built on the interpretive strategies and unique artistic
forms of African American culture, but also through engagement of specific African American textual antecedents. For example, *Bailey's Cafe*'s "signifying" on the Bible is intertwined with
its dialogue and revision of yet another (pre)text, Zora Neale
Hurston's *Moses, Man of the Mountain*.[40]

Since Alice Walker's discovery of Hurston as a literary grandmother, her texts have functioned as ancestral homeplaces or
points of literary origin for twentieth-century African American
women writers.[41] While some key tropes of Hurston's most famous novel, *Their Eyes Were Watching God*, resurface in *Bailey's
Cafe*, Naylor signifies on Hurston's retelling of the life of Moses
more directly. Signifying, as Henry Louis Gates Jr. has demonstrated, involves claiming, renaming, and ultimately revising aspects of the form and content of "black antecedent texts."[42]
Moses, Man of the Mountain dislocates the traditional Western
understanding of Moses by offering a "black re-reading" of his
struggles and powers informed by Hurston's study of Haitian
and African folklore.[43] Clearly, Naylor's revisions of Eve, Esther,
Mary, and Jezebel follow Hurston by asserting race as a fulcrum
of critique. The eruption of desire and its role in the construction of Naylor's own authority also has its roots in Hurston's
novel.

Moses inspired Hurston because she saw that the African legends exalting his power arose from his privileged discursive position. Anyone can follow God's commandments, but who, Hurston asks in the preface, "can talk with God face to face?" The conclusion of Hurston's preface links her explicit assertion of Moses' authority with an implicit assertion of her own. Moses' power:

did not flow from the Ten Commandments. It is his rod of power, the terror he showered before all Israel and to Pharaoh, and THAT MIGHTY HAND.

The Author

The thundering emphasis of "THAT MIGHTY HAND" and Hurston's immediate assertion of her own role as author suggest that the hand here metonymically represents Hurston's own writing and authority. Note, however, that the conclusion omits Hurston's signature, the linguistic sign of her gender.[44] This omission marks the territory that Naylor, guided by a hermeneutics of desire, attempts to remap in her novel.

Naylor signifies on Hurston's reimagination of biblical myth by insisting on gender and race as a double fulcrum, or a pivoting point of revision. Suspicious of the negative interpretations of Eve's sin or Jezebel's infidelity, Naylor sifts the original text, discerning a different story of immortal strength or stubborn independence. By contrast, Hurston's narrative evidences neither suspicion nor desire in its reimagination of female figures. Her portrayal of Miriam, for example, as a bitter, petty, false prophet detracts from that figure's significance in the biblical account.[45] Hurston's sole investment in Moses as God's agent or authoritative right hand may relate to another aspect of Naylor's signifying upon *Moses, Man of the Mountain*.

While Naylor departs from Hurston's focus on and identification with a powerful male biblical figure and instead reimagines several biblical women characters, she retains the posture of a male-identified, overarching narrator. Hurston's self-presentation as "The Author" is echoed and refigured in Naylor's self-presentation as "Maestro." Just as Hurston elides the gender of her individual signature, opting instead for a universal or generic title (and thus a masculine title in the tradition of Western literature), Naylor dons a male persona in the voice of the "Maestro," Bailey, who introduces and orchestrates the individual women's solos. Thus, both Naylor and Hurston cross gender lines in their figurations of their own authority.[46]

The significance of this act, though, is shaped differently by the historical contexts of each work. While Hurston's gender crossing evokes the traditional, universalizing construction of authority as gender-neutral, Naylor's gender crossing attempts to construct her authority as gender-plural. Bailey's own story opens the novel and functions in concert with the only other man's story, that of Miss Maple, to frame the chorus of women's stories. The two men's very different experiences of racism and World War II counter each other and implicitly offer a dialogue with the women's narratives on the theme of the construction of sexuality and identity.[47] Hence, Naylor's gender crossing reflects not a masking or evasion of the subject of gender, but an overt exploration of it in the womanist tradition that stresses the relation of gender and racial oppression.

Although, like *Moses, Man of the Mountain*, *Bailey's Cafe* asks who can talk face-to-face with God, the implied conversation between divinity and humanity in the latter takes a different shape. Naylor's reinvention of Eve through a hermeneutics of desire rests on an identification of the "spirituality" of the text with her own "sensuality," the corporeal reality of her own person that is inevitably shaped by gender, race, class, and sexual orientation, among other things.[48] It is perhaps this fundamental identification that allows the appropriation of biblical Logos evidenced by the prophetic language of Eve's interior monologue. The voice of biblical authority that emerges as Eve's own voice recalls the "Voice" of "I Am That I Am" which functions as character in Hurston's text. Despite the fact of his divine empowerment represented by his phallic rod, Moses' dialogue with God is characterized by the dramatic distance of conversation: Moses speaks and listens to the "Voice." In Naylor's text, however, this external dialogue is reconfigured as dialogic interplay. In other words, talking with God, or the authoritative discourse of the Bible, functions as a textual event in Hurston's novel but as an enabling (pre)text, or fundamental context for the creation of meaning, in Naylor's novel. As Morrison once commented, the "Bible wasn't part of my reading, it was part of my life."[49]

Notes

1. Gloria Naylor, *Bailey's Cafe* (New York: Harcourt Brace Jovanovich, 1992), section opening quote at 136. Hereafter, quotations from the novel are cited parenthetically in the text by page number.

2. Toni Morrison, *Song of Solomon* (New York: Plume, 1987). Further references to this edition will be noted parenthetically in the text by page number.

3. Naylor's biblical revision here functions like that of H.D., Alicia Ostriker, Jeanette Winterson, and other twentieth-century women writers whose work both contradicts traditional understandings of the Bible and simultaneously attests to new interpretive possibilities.

4. Adrienne Rich, *The Fact of a Doorframe* (New York: Norton, 1984), 319–324.

5. Susan Schweik, *A Gulf So Deeply Cut: American Women Poets and the Second World War* (Madison: University of Wisconsin Press, 1991).

6. See Alicia Ostriker's *Feminist Revision and the Bible* (Cambridge: Blackwell, 1993) on women's rewriting of the Bible, and see Rachel Blau Duplessis's *Writing Beyond the Ending: Narrative Strategies of Twentieth-Century Women Writers* (Bloomington: Indiana University Press, 1985) on women's rewritings of other canonical texts.

7. See, for example, the case of Sarah (Genesis 21.1–7) and of Rebekah (Genesis 25.19–25).

8. On the sources and process of the Bible's composition, see *The Literary Guide to the Bible*, eds. Robert Alter and Frank Kermode (Cambridge, Mass.: Harvard University Press, 1987). On the erasure of the feminine, see Ostriker, *Feminist Revision*, 33–38.

9. Margaret Homans, *Bearing the Word: Language and Female Experience in Nineteenth-Century Women's Writing* (Chicago: University of Chicago Press, 1986), 1–30.

10. Delores Williams argues that African American women's literature, by engaging patterns of representing African American women's sexuality, defines an area that feminist theologies must confront to understand the complexity of women's oppression in "Black Women's Literature and the Task of Feminist Theology," in *Immaculate and Powerful: The Female in Sacred Image and Social Reality*, ed. Clarissa W. Atkinson, Constance H. Buchanan, and Margaret R. Miles (Boston: Beacon Press, 1985).

11. Hortense Spillers, "Mama's Baby, Papa's Maybe: An American Grammar Book," *Diacritics* 17, no. 2 (summer 1987): 67.

12. Naylor begins her article "Love and Sex in the Afro-American Novel" (*Yale Review* 78, no. 1 [1989]: 19) with precisely this quote from Du Bois.

13. As Nancy Armstrong has argued in *Desire and Domestic Fiction* (Oxford: Oxford University Press, 1987), 31–35, novels that reveal the rhetorical operations of such contracts undercut fictions of essential identity. Following Louis Althusser, Armstrong stresses the function of the contract to regulate the identities of those who enter into it.

14. Ostriker, *Feminist Revision*, 18. She further explains that writers who reread the Bible with desire are projecting their concerns onto the text no more than any other exegete. Nor is the hermeneutics of desire a strictly feminist phenomenon; its creative dimension is intrinsic to all interpretation.

15. Karla Holloway defines this built-in plurality of meaning as a fundamental characteristic of African American women's novels in "Revision and (Re)Membrance: A Theory of Literary Structures in Literature by African-American Women," *African-American Review* 24, no. 4 (1990): 617–631.

16. See Ostriker's own revision of Freud, in which she claims that the "repressed of biblical narrative is evidently not the slain Father but the slain (and immortal) Mother" (*Feminist Revision*, 15).

17. See Bailey's interior monologue about World War II (23–26) and Sadie's internal reality of domestic order and security (72–76).

18. Ezekiel 16.6. I am indebted to Walter Reed for help in locating this passage and for turning my thoughts to Mikhail Bakhtin through his readings of biblical texts in *Dialogues of the Word: The*

Bible as Literature According to Bakhtin (Oxford: Oxford University Press, 1993).

19. Mikhail Bakhtin, *The Dialogic Imagination: Four Essays*, ed. Michael Holquist (Austin: University of Texas Press, 1981), 304.

20. Ibid., 344–346. Bakhtin also maintains that authoritative discourse, the "word of the fathers," is not double-voiced and thus cannot "enter into hybrid constructions" (342–344). While this may characterize the most extreme or perhaps ideal conception of authoritative discourse, the belief that writers' and readers' actual experiences of authoritative discourse can indeed be double-voiced is integral to my thesis.

21. See Homans's definition of representations of the Virgin with child as sites for remaking the meaning of bearing the Word (*Bearing the Word*, 30).

22. Brenda Marshall, "The Gospel According to Pilate," *American Literature* 57, no. 3 (1985): 486–489.

23. Ibid.

24. Phyllis Trible, "Love Lyrics Redeemed," in *The Song of Songs*, ed. Harold Bloom (New York: Chelsea House, 1988), 49–66, quote at 51.

25. Robert Alter, "The Garden of Metaphor," in *Song of Songs*, ed. Bloom, 121–139, quote at 139.

26. Ibid., 139.

27. See Ariel and Chana Bloch's description of the "friction" in the Song in *The Song of Songs: A New Translation* (New York: Random House, 1995), 6–7.

28. Alicia Ostriker, "A Holy of Holies: The Song of Songs as Countertext," unpublished manuscript, 16.

29. Trible, "Love Lyrics," 50.

30. Toni Morrison, "Rootedness: The Ancestor as Foundation," in *Black Women Writers (1950–1980): A Critical Evaluation*, ed. Mari Evans (New York: Doubleday, 1984), 339–345, quote at 343.

31. Houston Baker, *Blues, Ideology, and African-American Literature: A Vernacular Theory* (Chicago: University of Chicago Press, 1984), 7.

32. Ibid., 3–4.

33. Majorie Pryse, *Conjuring: Black Women, Fiction, and the Literary Tradition* (Bloomington: Indiana University Press, 1985), 9.

34. Henry Louis Gates Jr. defines the "speakerly text" as one "whose rhetorical strategy is designed to represent an oral literary

tradition" in *The Signifying Monkey: A Theory of African-American Literary Criticism* (New York: Oxford University Press, 1988), 181.

35. Voice here reflects the double-voiced tradition of African American literature since it functions as both an expression of individual identity and as a link to communal identity. See Gates's introduction, ibid., xxv. See also Morrison's comments in "Rootedness" on community voices (341).

36. Holloway, "Revision and (Re)Membrance," 622.

37. Ibid., 623.

38. Katie Canon, "The Emergence of Black Feminist Consciousness," in *Feminist Interpretation of the Bible*, ed. Letty M. Russell (Philadelphia: Westminster Press, 1985), 30–40, quote at 31.

39. Renita J. Weems, "Reading *Her Way* Through the Struggle: African American Women and the Bible," in *Stony the Road We Trod: African American Biblical Interpretation*, ed. Cain Hope Felder (Minneapolis: Fortress Press, 1991), 57–77.

40. Zora Neale Hurston, *Moses, Man of the Mountain* (1939; reprint, Urbana: University of Illinois Press, 1984). The strategic use of the Bible in slave narratives by nineteenth-century African American women may offer another interesting, if more distant, textual antecedent.

41. Alice Walker, *In Search of Our Mothers' Gardens* (San Diego: Harcourt Brace Jovanovich, 1983).

42. Gates, *Signifying Monkey*, 256.

43. Paola Boi, "Moses, Man of Power, Man of Knowledge: A 'Signifying' Reading of Zora Neale Hurston (Between a Laugh and a Song)," in *Women and War: The Changing Status of American Women from the 1930's to the 1950's*, ed. Maria Diedrich and Dorothea Fischer-Hornung (New York: St. Martin's, 1990), 115.

44. Nancy Miller discusses the effects of asserting or withholding the woman writer's signature in *Subject to Change: Reading Feminist Writing* (New York: Columbia University Press, 1988), 73.

45. Compare, for instance, Hurston's account of Miriam's role in the adoption of Moses (42–45) and as a leader of the Israelites (268–298) to the biblical account of her role in Numbers.

46. While some may see Morrison's use of a male protagonist in *Song of Solomon* in the same light, I do not think this argument really applies to that novel. Milkman is anything but a figure of authority and may fit better in the tradition of modern antiheroes.

47. In addition to contemporary attention to constructions of masculinity, the 1980's controversy about black women writers' portrayals of black men renders Naylor's male "Maestro" a politically useful writing strategy. See Deborah McDowell's discussion in "Reading Family Matters," in *Changing Our Own Words: Essays on Criticism, Theory, and Writing by Black Women*, ed. Cheryl Wall (New Brunswick, N.J.: Rutgers University Press, 1989).

48. See Ostriker's definition of this "erotic" identification and rereading (*Feminist Revision*, 66).

49. Toni Morrison, interview with Charles Ruas, ed., *Conversations with American Writers* (New York: McGraw-Hill, 1984), 215–243.

Conclusion

Last Words: Feminist Biblical Revision and Authority

The works of biblical revision examined in this study reveal that the most prominent themes in them—family relations, war, and audience—are all underwritten and connected by a single thread: the woman writer's quest to construct a different basis for her authority. From Emily Dickinson to Gloria Naylor, the engagement of biblical texts creates a context through which the woman writer's authority is articulated. In other words, the central subject of feminist biblical revision is not the Bible. Rather, it is the problems and possibilities of women's authority in a culture shaped by the masculine hegemony that the Bible has come to represent.

Nowhere is the woman writer's signature more evident or vexed than when it is made visible through dialogue with this founding text of Western culture. Recall the multiple and contradictory "I"s that address a divine pater in Dickinson's poetry. The struggle of this persona to define itself against, to be heard above, the Word of the Father seems emblematic of the publication history of Dickinson's work, the jagged path of her word toward less censored publication. Similarly, H.D.'s very signature—those hermetic initials—represent both her name and her naming by one of the chief representatives of the masculine literary tradition in the twentieth century. And finally, Naylor's figuration of her own authority as storyteller in the narrating voice of a male "Maestro" signifies both her bid for a classically magisterial voice and the cross-dressing implied by the performance of such a voice. This brief overview of these women writer's signatures illustrates how their position vis-à-vis the canonical literary tradition problematically shapes their authority.

Interestingly, feminist biblical revision seems to be spurred when the writer's authority is particularly pressured, either when a young writer is just designing her own signature or when a mature writer's sense of authority and vocation is undergoing transformation. Naylor's novel, for example, marks a period of literary apprenticeship, as the final work in a quarto assignment that Naylor set for herself as an exercise in her craft.[1] Both Sylvia Plath's and H.D.'s biblical revision, however, represent periods of transformation. Young but already technically accomplished, Plath wrote between 1960 and 1962 the poems that critics describe as her mature work. Indeed, the month that she drafted "Lady Lazarus" and "Ariel," letters to her mother confirm Plath's own sense of breakthrough: "I am a genius of a writer. I am writing the poems that will make my name."[2] *Trilogy* for H.D. similarly represented a breakthrough—the end of a long writer's block—and a transformation, a new relationship to language wrested from the crisis and destruction of war.

Some writers may turn to the Bible when their sense of authority or vocation is fragmentary or destabilized because of the strong association of that text with religious and literary authority. Perhaps because most feminist biblical revisionists are not practitioners of traditional organized religions, the literary dimensions of biblical authority are more readily defined in their work. "In the beginning was the Word" is both a challenge and a seduction to someone who feels her own word to be less than powerful. That famous beginning of John's Gospel offers an ontological story capable of conferring great power on the writer who can claim it as heritage. The writers in this study mine the treasured association of the Bible with authority in two related ways. Biblical authority often seems to function as a metaphor for literary authority, as when Dickinson figures her own word as divine communion or when Plath in her journal figures herself as "a righteous Eve . . . with the power of a desert prophet" upon receiving her first acceptance from *Harper's*. For all of these writers, however, the Bible also functions as a metonym for authority; as a cornerstone of the literary canon from John Milton to Herman Melville to T. S. Eliot, it is a part that, in a sense, represents the power of the whole.

Because of the problems, however, associated with reading women writers' signatures, the patrilineal authority of the Bible is not their literary legacy to inherit. Yet, as Dickinson's question "Why am I not Eve?" suggests, women writers' own embodied experience opens a door into textual interpretation and thus a way to stake a textual claim upon the tradition. As we saw in chapter 1, the feminist reform movement in the nineteenth century was often linked to interpretive battles over the Bible, and therefore the representational questions that accompanied "the woman question" were often grounded in the Word. The Word, then and now, functions as a site/cite for the woman question, for articulating female identity and authority. In this context, feminist biblical revision appears to be not only the revision of the Bible, but the revision of a discursive subject position. While this is a textual project, a remapping of a paper identity to produce more papers, it underwrites agency in the material world. Thus, feminist biblical revision is also "cultural work," in Jane Tompkins's sense of the term. *Trilogy's* response to war, *Song of Solomon's* resurrection of African mythology, and *Bailey's Cafe's* concern for racial and gender politics all have "designs" on their audience. But underlying these different foci is a common interest in home, the site of actual or figurative origins, as a locus of cultural work.

Throughout this study, I have used the term "home" because it evokes ideas of family, origins, and lineage that recur in these works. For the poets here, an especially charged authority emerges through their agon with a paternal figure: Dickinson, H.D., and Plath all do battle with the Word of the Father. The relative absence of a Word of the Mother, a feminine-gendered Logos, seems to call forth a different dynamic concerning maternal figures. H.D.'s Lady, Plath's ascending goddess, Toni Morrison's navel-less Pilate, and Naylor's immortal Eve all represent an imaginative conjuring of a female figure of the divine who heralds a different relationship of the woman writer to language. In a broad sense, Plath's youthful journal entry describing herself as the "Girl who wanted to be God" reflects the ambitious quest for creative power that is integral to every writer's sense of vocation but is too often discouraged in women writers because of misogynist injunctions against female self-assertion and authority.

Though the resurrection of a lost or buried goddess represents a liberating rewriting of "home" in the sense of literary origins, the works examined in this study also demonstrate that this revisionist enterprise is fraught with certain hazards to the woman writer's authority. The engagement of the Bible necessary to outline the traces of a repressed female divine figure requires a concomitant engagement of the tradition in Western literature of flesh loathing, particularly the dread of female flesh. As the disappearance of the goddess figure in the conclusions of Plath's poetry suggests, even the appropriation of characteristics of Christ can also lead to the adoption of a self-sacrificial rhetoric that dovetails disturbingly with traditional, misogynist rhetoric about women's roles and vocations. Similarly, while connecting actual family gender dynamics to a critique of a patriarchal hierarchy in representations of the divine can energize the writing of biblical revisionists, this trope too carries its own dangers. The work of Anne Sexton best exemplifies the hazards of the "home" trope, although similar dynamics appear in Plath's and even Dickinson's poetry. For Sexton, the all-powerful nature of the divine pater and the pervasiveness of the flesh-loathing tradition culminate in obliteration of the questing female speaker. Though the speaker finds God in the conclusion of *The Awful Rowing to God*, her "triumph" is also her extinction as she is consumed in his divine laughter.[3] Representing the divine through the traditional, unequal power distribution common in actual families may provide a telling critique of paternal power in religious and literary texts, but it may also mire the imagination in the problematic power dynamics of traditional families and churches.

The writing of an alternative "home" or literary place of origin into the biblical revision of *Trilogy*, *Bailey's Cafe*, and *Song of Solomon* offers a strategy for combating the problematic heritage inevitably evoked in a revision of patriarchal discourses. The mythological goddess traditions that H.D. calls forth function similarly to the African American musical and literary traditions that Morrison and Naylor summon. All provide an alternative ontological story of the writer's authority that balances or counters the power of the Word of the Father by drawing a different "Word" from other, marginal literary traditions.

While rewritings of home and literary lineage may be a logical or predictable focus of feminist literary revision, the significance of war in many of these texts may be surprising. Four out of five of the authors examined in this study make literary capital out of war: H.D. and Naylor confront war as subject matter, and Dickinson and Plath primarily use metaphors of war for other conflicts. As we saw in chapter 2, the use of war or battle as a trope for conflict with the Word of the Father reflects the oppositional nature of feminist biblical revision and the prevalence of the literary discourse of "arms and the man" in the canonical tradition also informed by the Bible. Like the "home" theme, war is also a locus for reformulating the relationship between gender and authority. Battle rhetoric invigorates Dickinson's struggle with a divine pater, whereas the double vision of the battlefield as Golgotha, the "place of a skull," energizes and ennobles H.D.'s quest to articulate a vision of gods and goddesses that would not underwrite war.

Naylor, like H.D., connects constructions of masculinity to war, but unlike H.D., she crosses the great gulf between war front and home front to give voice to a male soldier's combat experience. Rather than imagining the perspective of the soldier, Plath borrows imagery from the civilian victims of Nazi atrocity in the Holocaust. Thus, each writer's authority in these texts comes into being at least in part through taking an anti-war stance and making a critique of both the relationship of gender to war and the connection of the discourse of war to biblical tradition.

The link between the subject of war and revisionist authority, however, is complicated by several ties between "making war" and making texts. As we saw in chapter 1, greater access for women to social and economic opportunities during both World War I and II fostered a climate more conducive to all kinds of women's authority and self-representation, including literary representation. Tellingly, suffrage, women's political representation, was tied to World War I in Britain and America. Thus, it is not surprising that many feminists borrowed battle rhetoric, as Sandra Gilbert and Susan Gubar have shown in *No Man's Land*,[4] to express gender conflict. It is in this historical context that feminist biblical revisionists develop the pattern we first noted in Dickinson's poetry of agon with the Word of the Father. While the use of battle rhetoric, the threat to "eat men like air" that Lady Lazarus makes, may be problematic in its own right, it signals another hazard for the underlying project: the renegotiation of the woman writer's relationship to language. The inevitable ambivalence involved with taking an agonistic posture in an engagement with the Word of the Father can result in stagnant rhetorical structures, particularly the "X" of sous-ratour with its eternally opposed and unresolvable contradiction. This structure is most readily visible in the figure of feminine revenge that concludes "Lady Lazarus" and other Plath poems. The speaker's authority and power is simultaneously asserted and undercut by her status as victim. The subject of war, then, like that of home, is integral to the modification of a feminist writer's subject position in works of biblical revision, but it also brings its own dangers. No modification in the woman writer's subject position would be possible, however, without the special role of audience in feminist biblical revision.

Feminist biblical revision is fundamentally rhetorical, aimed to persuade an audience. Yet the role of audience in these texts is complicated by the fact that it encompasses not only the contemporary reader, but also the ancient text. In other words, these works are always addressing both an imagined or actual reader and a textual audience, the Bible itself. In chapter 1, we saw how Dickinson and H.D. drew upon the presence of actual female audiences, their companions, in shaping their addresses to the distant Word of the Father. In their situations, the intimate female audiences functioned as counters to the distant Word of the Father and fostered their reconstructions of authority. H.D.'s work, however, also articulates and draws power from an alternative textual audience in her resurrection of goddess traditions. Like the fostering personal audiences, this previously marginalized tradition sanctions the speaker's revisionist effort: the Lady "must have been pleased" that the searchers "did not forgo our heritage / at the grave-edge."[5] This resuscitation and construction of "heritage" marks a territory of audience that the novelists in this study also seek to map. The alternative literary ontologies or "homes" that Morrison and Naylor claim in African American literary and musical traditions perform the same function that the embodied, personal audiences did for the reconstruction of authority in the poets' work.

This strategic juxtaposition of audiences in feminist biblical revision is key to the modification of the woman writer's subject position, the renegotiation of "covenant" with which this study began. In feminist biblical revision, covenant—the contract between divine authority and humanity—is an appropriate symbol for the woman writer's relationship to authority in masculine-dominated discursive hierarchies, from Eliot's ideal order of literature to Jacques Lacan's symbolic order. Such systems draw on what Margaret Homans calls "the story of language," which predicates signification on a silent or absent female referent. By making a traditionally marginalized audience central and present, these personal and literary audiences *attend to* the renegotiation of the woman writer's relationship to authority: in short, they listen for a different story of language.

The difference in this story of language is perhaps most aptly articulated through a comparison with Mikhail Bakhtin's distinction between "authoritative discourse" and "internally persuasive discourse." Authoritative discourse is "the word of the fathers"; it is a "prior discourse," a "given" with its own "special language" not to be "profaned."[6] Clearly, the Bible has borne many of the traits of authoritative discourse. Internally persuasive discourse, in contrast, is a "word that is denied all privilege . . . and is frequently not acknowledged in society (not by public opinion, nor by scholarly norms, nor by criticism)."[7] Clearly, women's writing historically has borne many of the traits of internally persuasive discourse. For Bakhtin, authoritative discourse is rigid and inflexible, permitting "no play with borders," in contrast to the malleable and fluid quality of internally persuasive discourse.[8] However, Bakhtin does admit that in rare circumstances: "both the authority of discourse and its internal persuasiveness may be united in a single word—one that is *simultaneously* authoritative and internally persuasive—despite the profound difference between these two categories.[9]

I submit that feminist biblical revision offers just such a "word." The merger of authoritative and internally persuasive discourses, the "prior" Word of the Father and the contemporary word of the woman writer, is accomplished in part through the juxtaposition of audiences in feminist biblical revision. It is through the use of audience, along with the other strategies we have surveyed, that these writers renegotiate the covenant—the relationship between the woman writer and authority—and that, in Adrienne Rich's phrasing, "what's sacred tries itself / one more time."[10]

Notes

1. Naylor discussed this project she set for herself during a colloquium at Emory University, October 6, 1992.

2. Sylvia Plath, *Letters Home: Correspondence, 1950–1963*, ed. Aurelia Plath (New York: Harper and Row, 1975), 468.

3. Anne Sexton, *The Complete Poems*, ed. Linda Gray Sexton (Boston: Houghton Mifflin, 1981), 474.

4. Sandra Gilbert and Susan Gubar, *No Man's Land: The Place of the Woman Writer in the Twentieth Century*, 2 vols. (New Haven, Conn.: Yale University Press, 1988).

5. H.D., *Collected Poems, 1912–1944*, ed. Louis L. Martz (New York: New Directions Books, 1983), 568.

6. Mikhail Bakhtin, *The Dialogic Imagination: Four Essays*, ed. Michael Holquist (Austin: University of Texas Press, 1981), 342.

7. Ibid.

8. Ibid., 343–346.

9. Ibid., 342.

10. Adrienne Rich, "The Desert as Garden of Paradise," in *Time's Power, Poems 1985–1988* (New York: Norton, 1989), 25–31.

Select Bibliography

Alter, Robert, and Kermode, Frank, eds. *The Literary Guide to the Bible*. Cambridge, Mass.: Harvard University Press, 1987.

Annas, Pamela. *A Disturbance in Mirrors: The Poetry of Sylvia Plath*. Westport, Conn.: Greenwood Press, 1988.

Armstrong, Nancy. *Desire and Domestic Fiction*. Oxford: Oxford University Press, 1987.

Axelrod, Steven Gould. *Sylvia Plath: The Wound and Cure of Words*. Baltimore: Johns Hopkins University Press, 1990.

Baker, Houston. *Blues, Ideology, and African-American Literature: A Vernacular Theory*. Chicago: University of Chicago Press, 1984.

Baldwin, G. C. *Representative Women: From Eve, the Wife of the First, to Mary, the Mother of the Second Adam*. New York: Shelson, Blakeman, and Co., 1856.

Bennett, Paula. *My Life as a Loaded Gun: Female Creativity and Feminist Poetics*. Boston: Beacon Press, 1986.

Boi, Paola. "Moses, Man of Power, Man of Knowledge: A 'Signifying' Reading of Zora Neale Hurston (Between a Laugh and a Song)." In *Women and War: The Changing Status of American Women from the 1930's to the 1950's*, ed. Maria Diedrich and Dorothea Fischer-Hornung. New York: St. Martin's, 1990, 107–126.

Broe, Mary Lynn. *Protean Poetic: The Poetry of Sylvia Plath*. Columbia: University of Missouri Press, 1980.

Bundtzen, Linda. *Plath's Incarnations: Woman and the Creative Process.* Ann Arbor: University of Michigan Press, 1983.

Butscher, Edward. *Sylvia Plath: Method and Madness.* New York: Seabury Press, 1976.

Canon, Katie. "The Emergence of Black Feminist Consciousness." In *Feminist Interpretation of the Bible,* ed. Letty M. Russell. Philadelphia: Westminster Press, 1985, 30–40.

Clifton, Lucille. *Quilting: Poems, 1987–1990.* Brockport, N.Y.: BOA Editions, Ltd., 1991.

Cooper, Helen M., Adrienne Auslander Munich, and Susan Merrill Squier, eds. *Arms and the Woman: War, Gender, and Literary Representation.* Chapel Hill: University of North Carolina Press, 1989.

Dekoven, Marianne. *Rich and Strange: Gender, History, Modernism.* Princeton, N.J.: Princeton University Press, 1991.

DeLauretis, Teresa. *Technologies of Gender: Essays on Theory, Film, and Fiction.* Bloomington: Indiana University Press, 1987.

Dickinson, Emily. *The Complete Poems of Emily Dickinson.* Ed. Thomas H. Johnson. Boston: Little, Brown, 1960.

Diehl, Joanne Feit. *Dickinson and the Romantic Tradition.* Princeton, N.J.: Princeton University Press, 1981.

———. " 'Ransom in a Voice': Language as Defense in Dickinson's Poetry." In *American Women Poets,* ed. Harold Bloom. New York: Chelsea House, 1986, 23–39.

Duplessis, Rachel Blau. *The Pink Guitar: Writing as Feminist Practice.* New York: Routledge, 1990.

———. *Writing Beyond the Ending: Narrative Strategies of Twentieth-Century Women Writers.* Bloomington: Indiana University Press, 1985.

Eco, Umberto. *The Role of the Reader.* Bloomington: Indiana University Press, 1979.

Eliot, T. S. *Selected Prose of T. S. Eliot.* Ed. Frank Kermode. New York: Farrar, Straus, and Giroux, 1988.

Erkkila, Betsy. *The Wicked Sisters: Women Poets, Literary History, and Discord.* New York: Oxford University Press, 1992.

Foucault, Michel. *Discipline and Punish: The Birth of the Prison.* New York: Vintage, 1977.

Freidman, Susan Stanford. *Psyche Reborn: The Emergence of H.D.* Bloomington: Indiana University Press, 1981.

Freidman, Susan Stanford, and Rachel Blau Duplessis, eds. *Signet: Reading H.D.* Madison: University of Wisconsin Press, 1990.

Friedman, Ellen. "Where Are the Missing Contents?: (Post)Modernism, Gender, and the Canon." *PMLA* 108, no. 2 (1993): 240–252.

Froula, Christine. "When Eve Reads Milton: Undoing the Canonical Economy." *Critical Inquiry* 10, no. 2 (1983): 321–347.

Gates, Henry Louis, Jr. *The Signifying Monkey: A Theory of African-American Literary Criticism.* New York: Oxford University Press, 1988.

Gelpi, Albert. "Re-membering the Mother: A Re-reading of H.D.'s *Trilogy.*" In *Signet*, ed. Freidman and Duplessis, 318–335.

Gilbert, Celia. *Bonfire.* Cambridge, Mass.: Alice James Books, 1983.

Gilbert, Sandra. " 'A Fine White Flying Myth': The Life/Work of Sylvia Plath." In *Shakespeare's Sisters: Feminist Essays on Women Poets*, ed. Sandra Gilbert and Susan Gubar. Bloomington: Indiana University Press, 1979, 245–260.

———. "In Yeats's House: The Death and Resurrection of Sylvia Plath." In *Coming to Light: American Women Poets in the Twentieth Century*, ed. Diane Wood Middlebrook and Marilyn Yalom. Ann Arbor: University of Michigan Press, 1985, 145–166.

———. "Soldier's Heart: Literary Men, Literary Women, and the Great War." In Sandra Gilbert and Susan Gubar, *No Man's Land: The Place of the Woman Writer in the Twentieth Century.* 2 vols. New Haven, Conn.: Yale University Press, 1988, 258–323.

Guest, Barbara. *Herself Defined: H.D. the Poet and Her World.* New York: Doubleday, 1984.

Hall, Radclyffe. *The Well of Loneliness.* New York: Doubleday, 1928.

Hargrove, Nancy. "Christian Imagery in the Poetry of Sylvia Plath." *Midwest Quarterly* 31, no. 1 (1988): 9–28.

H.D. [Doolittle, Hilda]. *Collected Poems, 1912–1944.* Ed. Louis L. Martz. New York: New Directions Books, 1983.

———. *Tribute to Freud.* New York: New Directions Books, 1974.

———. *Trilogy.* New York: New Directions Books, 1973.

Holloway, Karla. "Revision and (Re)Membrance: A Theory of Literary Structures in Literature by African-American Women." *African-American Review* 24, no. 4, (1990): 617–631.

Homans, Margaret. *Bearing the Word: Language and Female Experience in Nineteenth-Century Women's Writing*. Chicago: University of Chicago Press, 1986.

———. *Women Writers and Poetic Identity: Dorothy Wordsworth, Emily Bronte, and Emily Dickinson*. Princeton, N.J.: Princeton University Press, 1980.

Irigaray, Luce. *This Sex Which Is Not One*. Ithaca, N.Y.: Cornell University Press, 1985.

Iser, Wolfgang. "The Reading Process: A Phenomenological Approach." In *Reader Response Criticism: From Formalism to Post-Structuralism*, ed. Jane Tompkins. Baltimore: Johns Hopkins University Press, 1988, 50–69.

Kroll, Judith. *Chapters in a Mythology: The Poetry of Sylvia Plath*. New York: Harper and Row, 1976.

Lant, Kathleen Margaret. "The Big Strip Tease: Female Bodies and Male Power in the Poetry of Sylvia Plath." *Contemporary Literature* 34, no. 4 (1993): 620–669.

Middlebrook, Diane. *Anne Sexton: A Biography*. New York: Random House, 1991.

Miller, Nancy K. *Subject to Change: Reading Feminist Writing*. New York: Columbia University Press, 1988.

Morrison, Toni. *Song of Solomon*. New York: Plume, 1987, 1978.

Naylor, Gloria. *Bailey's Cafe*. New York: Harcourt Brace Jovanovich, 1992.

Ostriker, Alicia Suskin. "The Americanization of Sylvia." In *Critical Essays on Sylvia Plath*, ed. Linda Wagner. Boston: G. K. Hall, 1984, 97–108.

———. *Feminist Revision and the Bible*. Cambridge: Blackwell, 1993.

———. "No Rules of Procedure: The Open Poetics of H.D." In *Signet*, ed. Freidman and Duplessis, 336–350.

———. *Stealing the Language: The Emergence of Women's Poetry in America*. Boston: Beacon Press, 1986.

———. "What Do Women (Poets) Want?: H.D. and Marianne Moore as Poetic Ancestresses." *Contemporary Literature* 27, no. 4 (1986): 475–492.

Perloff, Marjorie. "Icon of the Fifties." *Parnassus: Poetry in Review* 12–13, nos. 1–2 (1985): 282–285.

———. "The Two Ariels: The (Re)Making of the Sylvia Plath Canon." In *Poems in Their Place: The Intertextuality and Order of Poetic Collections*, ed. Neil Fraistat. Chapel Hill: University of North Carolina Press, 1986, 308–333.

Plath, Sylvia. *The Bell Jar.* New York: Harper and Row, 1971.

———. *The Collected Poems.* Ed. Ted Hughes. New York: Harper-Collins, 1992.

———. *Johnny Panic and the Bible of Dreams and Other Prose Writings.* London: Faber, 1979.

———. *The Journals of Sylvia Plath.* Ed. Frances McCollough. Consulting ed. Ted Hughes. New York: Dial Press, 1982.

———. *Letters Home: Correspondence, 1950–1963.* Ed. Aurelia Plath. New York: Harper and Row, 1975.

Pryse, Marjorie. *Conjuring: Black Women, Fiction, and the Literary Tradition.* Bloomington: Indiana University Press, 1985.

Ramazari, Jahan. " 'Daddy, I Have Had to Kill You': Plath, Rage, and the Modern Elegy." *PMLA* 108, no. 5 (1993): 1142–1154.

Rich, Adrienne. *On Lies, Secrets, and Silence: Selected Prose, 1966–1978.* New York: Norton, 1979.

———. *Time's Power: Poems, 1985–1988.* New York: Norton, 1989.

Ruland, Richard, and Malcolm Bradbury. *From Puritanism to Postmodernism: A History of American Literature.* London: Routledge, 1991.

Schussler-Fiorenza, Elisabeth. *But She Said: Feminist Practices of Biblical Interpretation.* Boston: Beacon Press, 1992.

Schweik, Susan. *A Gulf So Deeply Cut: American Women Poets and the Second World War.* Madison: University of Wisconsin Press, 1991.

Sexton, Anne. *The Complete Poems.* Ed. Linda Gray Sexton. Boston: Houghton Mifflin, 1981.

Smith, Martha Nell. *Rowing in Eden: Rereading Emily Dickinson.* Austin: University of Texas Press, 1992.

Spillers, Hortense. "Mama's Baby, Papa's Maybe: An American Grammar Book." *Diacritics* 17, no. 2 (summer 1987): 65–83.

Stein, Gertrude. "Composition as Explanation." In *A Stein Reader*, ed. Ulla E. Dydo. Evanston, Ill.: Northwestern University Press, 1993, 493–503.

Stimpson, Catherine. "What I Do When I Do Women's Studies." In *Literary Studies and Left Politics*, ed. Lennard Davis and M. Bella Mirabella. New York: Columbia University Press, 1990, 55–83.

————. *Where the Meanings Are: Feminism and Cultural Spaces.* New York: Methuen, 1988.

Tompkins, Jane. *Sensational Designs: The Cultural Work of American Fiction.* New York: Oxford University Press, 1985.

Van Dyne, Susan. "Fueling the Fire: The Manuscripts of Sylvia Plath's 'Lady Lazarus.' " *Massachusetts Review: A Quarterly of Literature, Arts, and Public Affairs* 24, no. 2 (1983): 395–410.

————. *Revising Life: Sylvia Plath's Ariel Poems.* Chapel Hill: University of North Carolina Press, 1993.

Wagner-Martin, Linda. *Sylvia Plath: A Biography.* New York: Simon and Schuster, 1987.

Walker, Cheryl. *The Nightengale's Burden: Women Poets and American Culture Before 1900.* Bloomington: Indiana University Press, 1982.

Williams, Delores. "Black Women's Literature and the Task of Feminist Theology." In *Immaculate and Powerful: The Female in Sacred Image and Social Reality,* ed. Clarissa W. Atkinson, Constance H. Buchanan, and Margaret R. Miles. Boston: Beacon Press, 1985, 88–110.

Wolff, Cynthia Griffin. *Emily Dickinson.* Reading, Mass.: Addison-Wesley, 1988.

Wolosky, Shira. *Emily Dickinson: A Voice of War.* New Haven, Conn.: Yale University Press, 1984.

Woolf, Virginia. "Thoughts on Peace in an Air Raid." *Death of the Moth and Other Essays.* New York: Harcourt Brace Jovanovich, 1942, 243–248.

————. *Three Guineas.* New York: Harcourt Brace Jovanovich, 1938.

Wurst, Gayle. " 'I've Boarded the Train There's No Getting Off': The Body as Metaphor in the Poetry of Sylvia Plath." *Revue Francaise d'Etudes Americanes* 15, no. 44 (1990): 23–35.

Young, James. " 'I May Be a Bit of a Jew': The Holocaust Confessions of Sylvia Plath." *Philological Quarterly* 66, no. 1 (1987): 127–147.

Zajdel, Melody M. " 'I See Her Differently': H.D.'s *Trilogy* as a Feminist Response to Masculine Modernism." *Sagetrieb* 5, no. 1 (1986): 7–16.

Index

About the Author

AMY BENSON BROWN is Visiting Assistant Professor of English at the State University of West Georgia. She has published several scholarly articles on women writers and coedited *The Reality of Breastfeeding: Reflections by Contemporary Women* (with Kathryn Read McPherson, Bergin & Garvey, 1998).